How to Romance the Woman You Love—The Way She Wants You To!

How to Romance
the Woman You Love—The Way
She Wants You To!

Lucy Sanna
with
Kathy Miller

PRIMA PUBLISHING

Production by Steven Martin
Copyediting by Kathryn Hashimoto
Interior design by Linda Shapiro
Typography by Archetype Book Composition
Cover design by The Dunlavey Studios
Cover photograph © Elizabeth Zeschin

Grateful acknowledgment is made to the following publications for permission to excerpt material:

Etiquette, by Emily Post, 1949, Funk & Wagnalls Company. New Revised *Etiquette,* 15th edition, © 1992 by Elizabeth L. Post. Reprinted by permission of Elizabeth L. Post and HarperCollins Publishers, Inc.

You Just Don't Understand, by Deborah Tannen, Ph.D. © 1990 by Deborah Tannen, Ph.D. By permission of William Morrow and Company, Inc.

The Power of Myth, by Joseph Campbell with Bill Moyers. © 1988 by Apostrophe S Productions, Inc., and Alfred van der Marck Editions. By permission of Doubleday, a division of Bantam Doubleday Dell Publishing Group, Inc.

Men Are from Mars, Women Are from Venus, by John Gray. © 1992 by John Gray. By permission of HarperCollins Publishers Inc.

The Road Less Traveled, by M. Scott Peck, M.D. © 1978 by M. Scott Peck, M.D. Reprinted by permission of Simon & Schuster, Inc.

Excerpts from *Intimate Play,* by William Betcher, M.D. © 1987 by William Betcher, M.D. Used by permission of Viking Penguin, a Division of Penguin Books USA Inc.

"People Are Hugging." Reprinted by permission of *The Wall Street Journal.* © 1993 by Dow Jones & Company, Inc. All rights reserved worldwide.

The Erotic Silence of the American Wife, by Dalma Heyn. © 1992, Dalma Heyn. By permission of Turtle Bay Books, a division of Random House, Inc.

Library of Congress Cataloging-in-Publication Data

Sanna, Lucy.
　　　How to romance the woman you love—the way she wants
　　you to / Lucy Sanna with Kathy Miller.
　　　　　p.　cm.
　　　Includes bibliographical references and index.
　　　ISBN 1-55958-664-8
　　　1. Love. 2. Intimacy (Psychology). 3. Man-woman relationships.
　　4. Marriage. I. Miller, Katherine Anne. II. Title
　　HQ801.S4336 1995
　　306.7—dc20　　　　　　　　　　　　　　　　　　94-36297

95 96 97 98 99 RRD 10 9 8 7 6 5 4 3 2 1
Printed in the United States of America

To Heinz,
who forgot that birthday

Contents

9. One-Minute Romancer 165

10. Your Romance Notebook 171

Acknowledgments

Because this book would not have become a reality without the help of many individuals, including creative advisors, reviewers, and general "cheerleaders," who supported and encouraged us through various stages of publication, we would like to thank everyone who lent an ear, an idea, or a red pencil along the way.

In particular, we give thanks to Larry Greene, Peter Jaret, Jay Kopelman, Stephanie Cincotta, Bob Kubik, and Janus Brush for their undivided attention—whenever we asked.

We also appreciate the honesty of hundreds of woman across the country who responded anonymously to our romance survey. Though we cannot thank you personally, we hope you know who you are. You provided the substance and credibility.

And thanks to computer whiz Tony Berumen, who kept us from crashing along with the hard disc. But for your magic touch, everything might have been lost.

Special thanks to Stan Vejtasa, who has provided romance every day through years of marriage, and Katie Frisch, who has supported her Mom through this and many other late-night writing projects.

Finally, we would like to thank Karen Blanco of Prima Publishing for championing the idea of this book. Her passion, dedication, and marketing acumen have carried us through.

We couldn't have done it without you.

The Authors

Introduction

In today's uncertain world—job layoffs, unsettling global affairs, natural disasters—we can easily feel overwhelmed by forces beyond our control. Nothing is stable. Nothing is sure. One place where men and women alike are turning for stability is to their love relationships.

While we can look back on the 1960s as "The Age of Free Love," the '70s as "The Age of Open Marriage and Divorce," and the '80s as "The Age of Reckoning," we can look to the '90s for healing.

In an attempt to understand what makes a relationship successful—in spite of today's life stresses and changing role models for both men and women—we developed a survey. In this survey, which focused specifically on the desires of women, we set out to discover the affirmations that might improve the chances of enduring love. And when we analyzed the responses—responses from women of all ages across the country—we found a consistency that validated the need for a book on the topic. To these affirmations we give the name "Romance."

From our research, we developed a powerful strategy for achieving and maintaining romance. It involves developing what we call a "romantic spirit." And in doing so, we look to the '90s as "The Age of Romance."

The focus here is on the romance that women desire in their love relationships. This is not to say that men do not desire romance, or that men do not have other needs that affect the relationship. Surely, that may be the topic for another book.

The Romantic Quest

Romance is as old as King Arthur's Court and as current as Hollywood.

Though individuals of either sex can seek a romantic spirit, the quest is particularly enigmatic for men today. Our male culture is currently beaten down with accusations of sexist attitudes, harassment, and bias. Because of all the controversy surrounding women's issues, a man might wonder how to please the woman he loves. Women want to be treated as equals, respected and trusted as corporate executives and Air Force pilots alike. But do they want romance? That men often feel confused about romance should not be surprising. Looking around at the new roles and identities women are choosing for themselves, men could easily conclude that treating a woman as someone special might even offend her.

Is there a place for romance? This certainly is an issue for a man who desires an enduring love relationship.

It did not surprise us to learn from our survey respondents that men put more effort into romancing a woman during the early stages of courtship. After a few years—or maybe even a few months—romance all too often goes into hibernation, making perfunctory appearances on anniversaries or other special occasions. We see couples moving together, but separately—unsmiling, hardly even looking at each other. The picture is unsettling. Are they in love? Is there tenderness? Communication? Intimacy?

Must stability bring an end to excitement? Is there a key to keeping a partner interested? Is it possible to renew the exhilaration, the vitality, or the romance of the early relationship? Is there a way to show the one you profess to love that you still and always care? Having compiled extensive data, we have determined that there is.

Though we'd like to think that a man wants to please the woman he loves simply for the sake of pleasing her, we learned from our research that if a man demonstrates certain romantic characteristics, he will certainly reap rewards.

Based upon our survey results, we can say with certainty that—unless a couple has major relational problems that require professional counseling—when a man becomes more romantic, his partner becomes more receptive to fulfilling *his* needs. Women consistently told us that they felt greater enjoyment from pleasing their partners after receiving the romantic attention they desired.

Women are individuals. There is no one secret, no simple trick, no silver bullet that assures a happy relationship. Instead, each man must find out what his own partner wants. The "secret" is that *there is no secret.* Know that and you will know what the true romantics know.

The concept is not a new one. In Geoffrey Chaucer's *Canterbury Tales,* written in Middle English in the fourteenth century, the Wife of Bath tells of a man's search for women's true desire. The man was "a lusty bacheler," one of King Arthur's knights, who was sentenced to death for ravishing a lovely maiden. But the ladies-in-waiting to the Queen pleaded for his life, and in response, King Arthur let the Queen decide his fate. She gave him a quest:

I grante thee lyf if thou kanst tellen me
What thing is it that women most desyren.

If he succeeded within a year and a day, he would be pardoned. Otherwise, he would lose his head.

Throughout the year-long quest, the young knight asked many women what they desired most, and he received many answers: wealth, honor, freedom, and pleasure were among them. But not one of these desires seemed to satisfy all women.

The day came when the knight had to return to the Queen. On the way home, he met a foul-looking woman sitting on the edge of a forest.

A fouler wight ther may no man devyse.

She told him she would give him the true answer if he would agree to do as she wished. He returned to the Queen with the answer:

Wommen desiren to have sovereynetee
As wel over hir housbond as hir love,
And for to been in maistrie him above.

Sovereignty over her love! None of the ladies could disagree with him, and the knight was pardoned. But then the old hag came to claim her side of the bargain: She wanted to be his wife. When the horrified young knight told her that he was repulsed by her looks, she gave him a choice: he could have her ugly and faithful, or she could change into a beautiful but faithless woman. In the face of such a terrible choice, he gave her sovereignty to choose. She then told him to kiss her, and when he did, she turned into a beautiful woman and swore to be faithful forever.

A thousand tyme a-rewe he gan her kisse,
And she obeyed hym in every thyng
That myghte doon him plesance or likying.
And thus they lyve unto hir lyves ende
In parfit joye . . .

Whether or not sovereignty is what all women want is not the point. Rather, the man gave his partner what *she* wanted. And in return, she fulfilled his desires.

Your own quest need not be such a struggle. But it will take some time, a little sleuthing, and most importantly, a lot of attention to your partner. Who is this fascinating woman? What gives her pleasure?

How to Romance the Woman You Love presents the results of a nationwide survey that shows what romance means to women in general. This gives you a basis upon which to begin. More importantly, however, *How to Romance the Woman You Love* provides a means for knowing your own partner's desires. Because that is the key.

The Romantic Spirit

From our survey we learned that women generally do not seek costly gifts or exotic trips. What a woman desires is a man who can bring romance to the every day—someone who always and everywhere lets her know that he appreciates her, respects her, makes her feel special.

Like the magician who can pull a dove from the air, the romantic man can create a mood—anywhere, anytime—just to please her.

Every woman is an individual. And there is no one formula a man can use to please all women. But there is a romantic attitude that any man can adopt to help decipher the mysteries of his partner's wishes—and fulfill her romantic desires. As Shakespeare once wrote, "They do not love who do not show their love." We call it a "romantic spirit."

From our survey, we learned that every woman needs to feel appreciated, wanted, and loved. Occasionally she even likes to feel indulged, "spoiled," and delighted with surprise. No matter how rewarding her everyday life, no matter how attractive, intelligent, and self-sufficient she is, she still needs caring and attention. Add a little romance to her life—it's such a simple thing if you know how—and watch the relationship evolve from something ordinary into something special.

From touching to keeping in touch, creating a romantic spirit can change your life.

We invite you to learn how easy it is to become a romantic— how easy to bring pleasure to the woman you love. It does not require a great deal of effort. It is actually very simple. And it is empowering for both partners.

Once you learn what romance is and how to make it happen, romance will become natural. A man practiced in romance finds opportunities everywhere. And as you grow your own romantic spirit, you will find new pleasure in your relationship—in the pure joy you receive in making your love happy, as well as in the pleasure you receive from her positive response to your new romantic attitude.

From anonymous responses to our survey, we found some fairly consistent views about what a woman wants in a relationship with the man she loves. Some of these desires may be beyond what a man is willing to give, and no woman would expect a man to fulfill every romantic whim. But even the smallest of romantic attentions can positively affect a relationship.

We discovered that there are certain things nearly all women expect in romance—on-going attentions that can take many forms. The specifics of romance may differ from woman to woman, but the central focus is always the same. As one survey respondent concluded: "As long as he shows me that he thinks I'm special—no matter where we are or what we're doing—that's romance."

Making her feel special—that's the bottom line. When you're with her, it's important that you're not just *next* to her, but that you engage her—in a very specific and special way—whenever you have the chance.

Growing Your Romantic Spirit

Not only did we ask women what they wanted, we also asked them how *well* their partner was satisfying their romantic needs. And what we found was that many otherwise *well-meaning* men don't have a clue as to how to please the women they love. Most men, it seems, do not realize how important romance is to women.

In response, we have developed an organized approach to romance: a step-by-step strategy to gain insight into what your partner desires and to grow your own romantic spirit. Whether you have just recently met that special woman or you've been with her for fifty years, you can play an instrumental role in bringing a new sense of romance to your relationship.

How to Romance the Woman You Love is based upon individual respect and, as such, it underlines the importance of learning a specific partner's needs as a prerequisite to pleasing her.

A hallmark of the book is the series of exercises offered in each chapter, giving you the opportunity right now to try out new attitudes and test new techniques—small steps that help you develop a more romantic spirit. The book asks you to devote a little more time and attention to your special woman. It asks you to be more sensitive to her needs. Doing so will not only bring new sparkle to your love relationship, but it can change *your* life—as well as that of your partner.

Start with the exercises and suggestions that are most comfortable for you. Test them. See how your partner reacts. Then try others that might be a little bolder, a bit of a stretch. And soon, to your delight, you'll begin to recognize your own romantic style; you'll begin to develop your own opportunities.

The final chapter presents you with a series of questions that will help you know what your own lovely lady desires. Once you have answers to those questions, go back through the exercises in the book and choose those most appropriate to your own situation. You might want to keep this book as a handy reference to return to now and again as you develop your capacity for romance.

In doing so, you'll see how easy it is to capture the romantic spirit. You'll find yourself changing in a way that's pleasing to her. And she'll respond in a way that's certain to be more pleasurable to you.

1

What Is Romance, Anyway?

Romance is the stuff of fairy tales, you say. Sure it is. And just as in those heroic tales, romance can create an escape into a pleasurable world in which any man can be the hero.

Have you ever allowed yourself to get swept up by an exciting story in a book or a movie? If the answer is yes, well, you already have a bit of the romantic in you.

Romance can create passion in a budding relationship, renew interest in a waning one, and bring excitement and surprise to one that has been going strong for years.

So what is romance, and how does a man go about becoming romantic?

Advertisements portray romance as a candlelight dinner at an expensive restaurant, or maybe a trip to Buenos Aires. But according to women surveyed, romance knows no time or place. It may not even cost you anything. Sure, a candlelight dinner or an exotic trip can have special appeal, but so can a walk in the rain or a picnic in the backyard—if you know how to make it romantic.

Romance is an attitude. An attitude that you create—anywhere. It involves sharing pleasures in such a way that lets your partner know she's special. It is being in the *present* with the one you love, sharing whatever it is you are doing, creating joy. Something as small as a wink, a smile, or a touch can set it in motion. And *voila,* you're a romantic!

Just to prove it to yourself, go to a restaurant and watch couples eating together. The food, the music, the decor is the same for them all, but you'll see a great variety of attitudes: one couple is arguing; another may be distracted by people around them; while a third couple is totally engrossed in each other, looking into each other's eyes, sensuously feeding each other and licking each other's spoons. Which couple enjoys the best romance?

You may be watching the most beautiful sunset, but if you don't have that romantic attitude pulsating between you, you might as well be alone. On the other hand, though the setting may be irrelevant, you can learn to make use of your surroundings to help create a romantic mood.

Though feelings about romance may differ from woman to woman, the central focus is always the same. As one of our survey respondents concluded:

> The surroundings don't matter. We could be at the top of the Eiffel Tower or in the mall shopping for diapers. But when his attention shows me that he appreciates my uniqueness, that's romantic.

Moreover, romance is cumulative, like an investment. It compounds itself over time. With each small romantic moment, the relationship grows more romantic as a whole. Women remember romance.

Of course, romance is not just for women. From all indications, men like to be romanced, too. But if you start, she's sure to follow.

Creating Romance Anywhere

In our survey, we asked, "Has there been a time when a partner has made you feel really special?" This sampling of responses should help you discover what women find romantic.

We were visiting my parents. It was a bright cold winter day. We grabbed some old ice skates out of the garage and walked down the street to the lake where I had often skated as a girl. I sat down on the bench and was about to change into my skates when he squatted down in front of me and gently drew off my boots. And then he helped me into my skates and laced them up for me. Of course he knew I could do this perfectly well myself. But that's what made it romantic. And that's when I knew I was in love with him.

We found great variety in the settings women find romantic. Where one preferred a warm cozy fireplace and a big tub with bath oils, another yearned for a campfire and a mountain stream. But the ingredients for romance remained the same: "He knows what I enjoy and he's taking time and giving attention to enjoying it with me."

This idea came up again and again. As one woman wrote:

Flowers can be very romantic in the right situation, and a turn-off in another. Spontaneous sex can be fun and playful if you feel well rested, but not if you're exhausted or feel unappreciated. Just about anything can be romantic if a relationship has an ongoing sparkle. It is not the specifics that make things romantic so much as the awareness in a close relationship that heightens the romance of the smallest things—a touch on the shoulder, for example, or holding hands.

It didn't matter where they were or what they were doing; if their partner was giving them attention on an ongoing basis, then romance happened. And the romance that came out of such moments was remembered. Cumulative.

Creating Romantic Backgrounds

If the attitude is right, fire can enhance romance like nothing else: candles, bonfires, fireplaces . . .

It was snowing and he went out to the porch to chop some wood. He carried in the logs and set them in that organized way of his and made the most beautiful fire. I love to watch him chopping wood and making a fire. It's such a sensual primitive act. Even though I'm capable of doing it myself when he's not around, he's never more masculine than when he's building a fire for me.

Combine firelight with special attention, and you've got the makings for romance.

One particular evening early in our marriage, we had showered and were sitting in our bathrobes in front of the fire. He took my brush and brushed my hair. Long slow strokes. I could tell that he really enjoyed playing with my hair. The feeling was so luscious, I remember it still.

Water can be relaxing as well as sensual: picnicking by the riverside, swimming in a pool, strolling along the shore in the moonlight.

He asked me to meet him at the aquarium. The low lights, the fish swimming languidly through deep green water. His face came up behind me in the reflection of the dolphin tank. He smiled toward me in the glass. Irresistible. Watching those lovely gray and white bodies swimming gracefully before us. We gave them all names and made up stories as if they were characters in a great drama. I was infatuated.

Other forms of nature bring their own mystery: hiking through the woods, biking along a country road, sharing a glass of wine in front of a setting sun. If you are paying attention to *her,* just being together in a scenic spot gives you the backdrop for a romantic event.

Surprising Her

Spontaneity brings a special kind of excitement. Spontaneity comes naturally for some men, but for others it takes a bit of forethought and creative planning. What makes her smile? What causes laughter? What would make her brag about your relationship to her friends?

Letting her know that you care every day—not just on special occasions—is sure to get her attention.

I came home from work one night and opened the refrigerator to pull out whatever there might be for dinner. And there on the second shelf next to the leftover chicken was one beautiful long-stem white rose with a note that read "Thought of you today." He must have come home sometime during the day just to put it there.

But you can delight her with surprise anywhere.

We were driving in an unfamiliar area on our way to an art exhibition I had wanted to attend, when we realized we were totally lost. Experience with past relationships told me to brace myself for the offense: Why didn't I get better directions, why didn't I bring the map, etc. etc. etc. The day was hot and sticky and I was wishing we had never left home. Suddenly we came upon a lovely little lake and he said "C'mon, hon, let's go for a swim." Just like that. It was such an unexpected proposal. So we stripped and dove in and I'll never forget it.

Pampering Her

Simple pleasures, thoughtfulness. The smallest acts are often the most cherished. It doesn't matter whether you've been married to her for fifty years or you've just met—anything you do to pamper her will certainly be appreciated.

When he stays over on weekends he makes coffee while I'm in the shower. It's a small thing, but it's such a treat to have him hand me that warm cup as I emerge from behind the curtain. And I've never told him this but on the mornings in between, when he's not around—when I make my own coffee—I think of the wonderful times we've had and look forward to our next lovely weekend together.

Noticing Her

Paying attention to how your partner looks has its own rewards. In fact, it's the best way you can let her know that you desire her. And if she knows you desire her physically, it helps her feel more relaxed with you and less inhibited. So tell her now. Even if she's a brilliant Nobel Prize winner and she knows that you're attracted to her for her intelligence, don't forget that she's also a woman. And tell her what it is about her physically that turns you on. Be specific. Tell her again and again.

There is nothing more romantic than a man who loves women—loves the way their bodies look, the way they smell, the way they move.

> When I'm leaving for work in the morning, he compliments me on my looks—not just "You look good," but details. He tells me about how the color I'm wearing brings out my eyes or how creative I am in putting together an outfit. And sometimes he says how he envies the men I'll be with at the office. It makes me feel sexy and excited for him. It makes me more interested in looking good for him. And then when I arrive home from work before he does, I change my lingerie so that when I strip off that dress he watched me put on in the morning I have my sexy little things on underneath—just to please *him*.

Being Private

Being private in public can add a certain naughtiness to romance for some women. But you've got to know your limits. Some women were brought up with the notion that men should only hold an elbow to help steer a course across a busy street. Others enjoy holding hands. Still others go all out: arm around the shoulder, around the waist, a stolen kiss, well . . . How about your special woman?

> When we're at one of my business functions, I love it when he looks at me in a way that says "I can't wait to get you home." It's

such a pleasurable sensation to feel desirable in a crowd that thinks of me in only professional terms.

Sharing Sensual Pleasures

Shared pleasures can be oh-so-romantic. Eating is one sensual pleasure that anyone can enjoy more when sharing:

> I fell for him on our second date. He took me to a terrific restaurant for dinner. He ordered the lamb, and then after he tasted it he smiled and held a forkful up to *my* mouth—it seemed so natural, that sharing. And then he nonchalantly reached across the table and poked his fork into my fish and I felt so—I don't know—so *one* with him. It was such a delight. Soon we were feeding each other from his plate, from my plate . . . it was so sensual. I was ready for anything!

All the senses can respond to nurturing. And when it happens, women remember:

> I arrived at the airport in the morning after a 20-hour flight. He was there, waiting with a kiss. He picked up my luggage and brought me home. I was exhausted. I looked a mess. He told me I was beautiful. He ran a bath. He bathed me with perfumed soap. He washed my hair. He wrapped me in a clean white towel. He tucked me into sweet-smelling sheets. And when I woke in the afternoon, he handed me a glass of champagne. "Welcome home, baby," he said. Oh yes! So glad to be home.

Touching Her

Touching—anywhere, anytime—keeps her wanting you. One of the most important findings from our survey was that women want to be touched more. When asked to rate the statement "He touches me with tenderness," ninety percent of survey respondents answered that this was *very important*, and ninety-three percent said that it did not occur often in their relationship. Romantic men, take note.

When we're sitting together in the movie theater and he puts his arm around me—no matter what argument we had last night or what trouble the kids got into that afternoon or how bad my day was at the office—I forget it all and just melt into his embrace. He wants me there with him. And I want to be with him. And that feeling lasts.

Another way to touch is through clothing and jewelry:

Sometimes he sees me trying to put a bracelet on with one hand, or trying to clasp a necklace behind my back. "Here, let me," he says. I don't know why, but his touch at these times—just the brush of his fingers against my wrist or my neck—is so exciting.

Keeping in Touch

Keeping in touch when you are apart from each other can bring you closer together. Women believe that they think of their partner much more often than their partners do of them. Whether this is perception or reality (let's leave that for another study), rest assured that if you let her know you do think of her, she'll feel more confident of your mutual relationship. You can communicate in many ways: letters, phone calls, even little messages via electronic mail.

I still remember a postcard from an old lover back in college. He went off to the Peace Corps for the summer. I don't remember the entire message, but the important part goes something like this: "Incredibly intense . . . fast-paced . . . continual sleep deficit . . . no time to think . . . but somehow find myself thinking of you. Saw you in my dreams last night." Everything about him was so romantic. I thought of him always. And though I've gone on with my life and I haven't seen him in over fifteen years, I think of him still.

Even when the distance between you is only an emotional one . . .

After I broke off with a boyfriend, he left a single rose on my doorstep every day for nearly three months. It wasn't because of the roses that I eventually took him back, but because he was serious about keeping me in his life.

Paying Attention to Her Ideas

Too often, women believe they are not heard. Giving time and attention to your partner's thoughts and ideas can add romance to your relationship. If she's your partner, you can be her hero. Speak up and help her give her ideas the airing they deserve.

We were at a small dinner party. The couple giving the party had just moved into a new house and was concerned about landscaping, and everyone was offering suggestions. I threw out an idea but it was not picked up. After a few more minutes of conversation my husband said, "Leslie had a good idea about shading the back patio." And the table immediately took up my idea and discussed it seriously. He made me feel appreciated. That's something that I've now learned to do for him, as well.

Participating in Family Matters

If you have children—hers from a previous relationship or yours together—she'll appreciate any special effort you make on their behalf. Issues surrounding care-giving are often sensitive ones, particularly regarding time and energy spent. And unless you're a teacher, a therapist, or a really special guy, you probably have no idea what physical, emotional, and psychological energy goes into rearing those children. But if you are there to help, well, then you are special in her eyes.

The lights went out in the storm. He got the flashlight and read stories to the children, making it an adventure, assuring them that everything was ok. And when they fell asleep, he carried them off to bed. Then, to my delight, with the storm blowing all around us,

he turned off the flashlight and lit candles. And in that soft romantic light, he read *me* the children's stories—only now he read them
as if they were erotic, adding lusty little comments between the
lines. When the electricity came back, he turned off the lights, leaving the soft candlelight. The next day the neighbors were talking
about the problems that came from the storm. But for me, thinking
back on that lovely time, well, it's just another reminder of why I
love him so much.

Planning Special Events

Women love the romance of intimate trysts, whether planned
or spontaneous. Your partner will surely thank you if *you* initiate the time out.

I was thrilled to receive an invitation in the mail one day. It was
from my husband, inviting me to share a day off with him the following Friday. Unheard of! He had arranged for the children's favorite baby-sitter to come early—even before the kids were
up—and then stay late so that we could spend the evening together, as well. We started the day by going out to breakfast—no
rush, no hurry, no interruptions (wonderful!)—and ended it dancing at one of the local night clubs. In between, we enjoyed window
shopping, lolling in the park, and a leisurely romantic dinner. It
was so good to get away and be just the two of us for a change. I
felt closer to my husband than I had for years. And after that little
time out, I felt I had more energy for the kids, as well.

Including Her in Your Life

Including the woman you love in aspects of your own life—in-
troducing her to your friends, inviting her to your work-related
social events, showing her a place that is special to you, teaching her a new hobby or skill—can only bring you closer. Three
examples:

That first time he included me in his Saturday outing with his son,
well, I knew I was special to him.

My current partner likes to go camping with his friends, and at the beginning of our relationship, it meant that he was away many weekends. I was both apprehensive and excited one day when he invited me to go along. I didn't know anything about camping. But I had such a good time and learned that I can actually put up a tent and fish and then sleep through the night with little critters prowling around. I appreciate that part of his life now and understand why it's so important to him. He still goes off with his buddies once in a while, but it's something that we can share alone together as well.

My husband travels occasionally, but he always said it was morning-to-night business and he wouldn't have any time for me if I went along. Besides, we can't afford a lot of frivolous vacations. But one Wednesday, as he was leaving for New Orleans—a city he knew I wanted to visit—he handed me an airline ticket to meet him Friday afternoon at his hotel. He had already arranged to take Monday off and so we had a fabulous long weekend together. He has since joined an airline mileage plan so that when he earns free miles I can travel with him. And we're looking forward to more fun times together.

Participating in Her Life

More than one woman said she would love her partner to take part in things in which he has no interest— just because she is interested. This means letting her share her interests, her work, and her hobbies.

Before I met Paul, I rode my bicycle a lot—weekend campouts, metric centuries, club rides. But when Paul and I started dating, there just wasn't any time for that. We had other things to do— mostly things he enjoyed that he got me interested in as well. And my bike hung on the garage wall like a relic. One day I mentioned to him that I missed riding my bike on weekends, and I got really passionate about it. I guess he realized how important it had been to me, because a few weeks later, he came over with his new bike and said, "Where do you want to ride today?" Now I've got Paul *and* my bike . . . I've got everything I want. And the good news is that he's enjoying this new sport as much as I am.

Playing an Age-Old Game

Definitions of romance come to us through scholarly historical and anthropological texts. In his book *The Power of Myth,* Joseph Campbell, Jungian anthropologist, speaks of the five virtues of the medieval knight: Temperance, Courage, Love, Loyalty, and Courtesy. According to Campbell, the idea of romance began with courtly love in twelfth-century Provence, France:

> It was a very strange period because it was terribly brutal. There was no central law. Everyone was on his own, and, of course, there were great violations of everything. But within the brutality, there was a civilizing force, which the women really represented because they were the ones who established the rules for this game. And the men had to play it according to the requirements of the women.
>
> The essential idea was to test this man to make sure that he would suffer things for love, and that this was not just lust.

And what does all this mean for the modern man? From written comments from survey respondents, we can define a romantic attitude as a respect for a loved one's needs and desires. If a man respects the woman he loves, he will pay attention to her needs and aim to fulfill her desires.

As you read through the chapters that follow—and learn what hundreds of women across the country have said they *really* want—think about integrating some of these ideas into your own love relationship.

Start with the ones that are most comfortable for you, and later choose other exercises that might be a little newer, a little riskier. After a while you'll begin to recognize opportunities for romance all around you. You'll see how easy it is to become romantic, naturally. And you'll find that to "suffer things for love" can actually be a lot of fun for you as well as for her.

For starters, try some of the simple exercises that follow, and start seeing immediate results.

Activities to Hone Your Romantic Spirit

Following are examples of actions and activities which, according to our survey respondents, express the romantic spirit. Try one or two now, and then come back later for more when you feel comfortable enough to take a few more risks.

- Use her name—or a special "love name"—when speaking with her. Try using her name every time you say hello and good-bye, and at least once during each conversation. If you are already in the habit of doing this, do it even more often.
- Call her up in the middle of the week (or sometime when she wouldn't expect it) and invite her out to dinner (yes, even if you're married!). If that evening is not good for her or if she must make special arrangements ahead of time, don't be discouraged (this may be as new to her as it is to you); offer another day.
- Bring her a surprise gift for no special reason. When she asks you why, you might tell her you've been thinking about how special she is to you. Try one of the following:
  1. A single rose (ring the doorbell and hand it to her, leave it for her to find in the refrigerator, or put it into a vase and present it when you both sit down for dinner)
  2. A small piece of jewelry or other personal item she admired when you were shopping together (wrap it nicely, put it into a decorated gift bag and hand it to her, or hide it in her lingerie drawer)
  3. A love note (send it in the mail or hide it where only she will find it)
- Call her in the middle of the day for no reason but to say that you're thinking of her. Ask how her day is going. If

she asks you about yours, let her know that you only want to talk about her right now. And listen to what she says. Make mental notes about any concerns or desires she may mention.

- Touch her regularly in nonsexual ways. Kiss her when you greet each other, even in public (lightly on the cheek is fine). Kiss her when you part. Hold her hand when crossing the street. Touch her shoulder or arm during conversation. Take her arm when you're walking together down the sidewalk or even down the grocery aisle.
- When she least expects it, look her directly in the eyes and tell her you love her.
- Thank her the next time she does something that she routinely does for you without thanks.
- Give her a meaningful compliment—either on the way she looks or on something she's accomplished. Be specific. Instead of "You look great tonight," try "That color brings out the wonderful blue of your eyes," or "Your hair smells so lovely tonight," or "I've always loved your (*fill in the blank*)." Don't make up something just to say anything; tell her only what you truly believe.
- Run a bath for her—just the way she likes it, with oils or bubble bath or water softeners. Put a candle in the bathroom and a cup of tea or whatever she'll like. Get anything she wants or needs—a drink refill, a different soap, etc. Offer to wash her back or shampoo her hair. Hold her towel ready when she's finished and gently, slowly towel her down.
- Begin to notice what she asks for. See if you can decipher some of her nonverbal clues as well as her verbal ones.

2

Women's Romantic Desires

What do woman want today?

From hundreds of responses to a survey about romance we found some pretty consistent views about what a woman wants in a relationship with the man she loves. The demographics of survey respondents ranged all over the map: single, divorced, widowed, married; from ages 20 to 75; from high-school diploma to Ph.D.; from all regions of the country. And among them, they have a breadth of experience with men that bears note. Their anonymous responses reveal more than a little about what pleases women today.

The bottom line: Women want affirmation.

If you don't let your partner know that she is special to *you*, there is no romance. Even if your partner is a million-dollar runway model, an Olympic athlete, or a Pulitzer Prize winner, she wants affirmation from you that she is accomplished, beautiful, and fascinating. But if you don't let her know what in particular you appreciate about her—if you don't *affirm* her specialness—then telling her that she is special is just so many words. It only means that you have not thought about her enough to articulate her uniqueness.

Women told us that they want to feel loved, appreciated, and respected for who they are. Just acting on that small bit of information could turn a relationship around.

Now if you're thinking that *women* need to do a better job of romancing you men, well, don't despair. Let this book provide the insight into beginning the process toward a more romantic relationship for both of you.

Fewer than half the women surveyed told us they had enough romance in their relationship. When queried about what their reaction would be if their partners were more romantic, seventy-five percent of survey respondents replied that they would give a man's needs more attention if he were more attentive to theirs. Written comments underline the fact that this is definitely not a tit-for-tat bartering but, rather, a change of attitude in the relationship itself. Even those women married for years say they themselves would change in light of a new romantic spirit.

So how do you go about becoming more romantic?

The first step is to pay attention. Giving your partner attention does not mean merely sitting next to her on the couch when you watch TV. It means noticing her, appreciating her, engaging her in your life—and you in hers. And when you notice something beautiful, unique, or charming about her, tell her—either with words or with your actions. If her hair is beautiful to you, for example, touch it, brush it, play with it. Not only will this new attitude turn a ho-hum relationship into a sparkling romance, but it will also go a long way to help her feel better about herself.

In his book *The Road Less Traveled*, M. Scott Peck states,

> The principal form that the work of love takes is attention. When we love another we give him or her our attention; we attend to that person's growth. When we love ourselves we attend to our own growth. When we attend to someone we are caring for that person. The act of attending requires that we make the effort to set aside our existing preoccupations . . . and actively shift our consciousness.

The woman you love wants you to find her fascinating. She wants you to explore her like a new country. Even if you've slept beside her for years, there are so many things about her that you don't know. Get her to open up about her dreams, her fantasies, her goals.

Romantic needs are not difficult to fulfill. With a little practice—and a little perseverance—any man can master them.
Don't give up if she does not respond as quickly or as intensely
as you would like; after all, if this is new to her, she's got to
watch you a bit to learn the rules before she can begin to play
with confidence. On the road to establishing your romantic
spirit, note her reactions—the signposts along the way—and
trust that becoming romantic will bring your partner closer to
you, allowing you a deeper and more fulfilling relationship.

One of our happier respondents told us her partner's secret:

> The man I love seems to know ahead of time what I want. I told
> him once that he must be psychic. But he said that for a number of
> years he was a salesman and he learned how to notice what his
> clients needed. Sometimes he asks little questions, sometimes he
> just observes. He says that, now, that capability is integrated into
> his personality and it's just a way of life for him. It's not that he's try-
> ing to sell me anything, he just knows how to please me because
> he wants me to be pleased.

Learn as much as you can about that woman you love. Give
her at least as much attention as the customer you are wooing.
Find out what she wants, and then fulfill her romantic needs.
Chapter 10, "Your Romance Notebook," will help you discover
your own partner's romantic desires.

Verbalize Your Appreciation

I do appreciate her," you may say, "and I know that she knows
it."

Well, maybe she does, and maybe she doesn't. But according
to our survey respondents, she wants to *hear* it.

Love Her for Who She Is

A man doesn't need to have an athlete's body, a movie idol's
face, or a bank chairman's purse to be a romantic. And a

woman doesn't need to be glamorous to want romance. She doesn't need to be a goddess, a queen, or a Fortune 500 CEO to deserve respect, appreciation, and applause. She is charming for who she is. Let her know that. Reinforce her strengths. Celebrate her accomplishments. Appreciate her true self.

You can create a strong romance by letting your partner know that you appreciate the many things—large and small— that make her your love. Among others, these may include her sense of humor, her organizational qualities, her artistic capabilities, her ease with conversation, her capacity for nurturing and motherhood, her thoughtfulness, her sensitivity, her sexual capacity—whatever it is that you appreciate about her.

The best way to let her know is to tell her.

If you've never put such feelings into words, think about her assets—write them down, if you must—and choose among them to appreciate one today, another tomorrow, and a different one next week.

We received many survey responses from women who felt unappreciated. But, according to one of our respondents, here's how it can work:

> I'm very lucky because I know I have a special relationship with my husband. When we're having a good time, he tells me I'm so much fun to be with. When we're talking, he repeats what I say as if he values it and wants to remember it. And when we're making love, he tells me again and again how sexy I am. So even if I've had a bummer day at work, I can come home to him to feel fun and smart and sexy.

Appreciate What She Does

Whether she spends her time working out of the house or maintaining the household, she does so many things during the day without comment, without recognition. Don't take anything for granted. Notice what she does and tell her where she's most capable. Maybe she can persuade the PTA, manage the bills, or redecorate the living room. When she does something well—whether it's something she does for the first time or something she has been doing for years, and whether it's trivial or earthshaking—praise her for it.

And don't forget to thank your partner for what she does for you, from making your bed to making your dental appointment. Find at least one thing per week for which to thank her, and you will find the pleasure in your relationship growing—for both of you.

Some of the sweetest things he has done for me are those that tell me he appreciates who I am. He gives me a card or poem on each of our children's birthday, thanking me for giving him his family. He brags to his brother, who is in debt, about how well I manage the finances. And whenever I try something new, he's always there to encourage me and give me strokes for the effort even if the final product is not the best. His support and encouragement help me to feel capable and, well, loved. I think that's one of the reasons that our relationship has stayed vital and romantic for so many years.

Recognize Her Genius

She wants you to recognize that she has creative ideas, useful advice, and maybe even witty conversation—basically, that she's nothing short of wonderful. She may offer an idea, perhaps related to your home, to your wardrobe, or to your work; instead of simply accepting it—or, worse yet, brushing it aside—tell her you appreciate it.

When you have a problem in need of a solution, share it with her. Give her the opportunity to think it through with you. Most importantly, consider carefully everything she offers.

Affirm Her Beauty

Madison Avenue, with its multitake commercials and air-brushed magazine ads, has set a beauty standard that few women can attain. Even though your partner may not measure up to the "air-brushed" standard, she has many physical qualities that you love.

Let her know that for you she is the most beautiful woman on earth.

Instead of simply saying, "you're beautiful," however, which she may or may not believe, point out something special about the way she looks right now: "That dress brings out your terrific shape." "Your hair shines brilliantly in this light." "I love the way your eyes laugh when you smile."

Know her.

Start noticing the way she looks—the details: the energy of her walk, the shine in her eye, the beauty that endears her to you. You've accepted this without comment for too long. Begin verbalizing what it is about her that excites you, causes you to stop and look, stays in your mind later. Tell her now, when you notice it, and tell her later, when you call her: "I've never told you how I love to feel your hair . . . it's so soft." The strength in her thighs, the scent of her skin, the color of her eyes, the little curl that hangs on her neck. Whatever it is, make it personal and true.

And the more you train yourself to notice, the more loving comments you will be able to share with her. And then watch your romance soar.

You'll get *special* points if you verbalize what you notice when other attractive women are in the room. Just putting your arm around your partner's waist and whispering "I'm so glad I'm with *you* tonight" will do wonders for your romance.

One of our happier respondents told of her experience with a romantic:

When we first got married, he made me nervous, always watching me. He watched me when I got dressed for work, when I got undressed, while I set the table or made the bed or talked on the phone. I was always thinking that he was noticing all my faults—my heavy thighs, my straight wet hair, my hanging breasts. But when I told him he was making me nervous, he started telling me what he saw—your "sweet round tush," your "sly smile," your "round breasts." And now when he watches me, he tells me those little details that make me want to show off for him. He makes me feel beautiful.

If your partner happens to *ask* you about her appearance—her hair, her dress, whatever—use diplomacy in your answer. Find something nice, something that you can honestly appreciate: "That dress brings out the color of your beautiful eyes." "Your new haircut shows off your high cheekbones." "Sexy legs." But be truthful. As one of our survey respondents wrote:

> When he wants to let me know that I just don't look good in something, instead of saying so and making me feel less than beautiful, he tells me that something doesn't flatter me—the dress doesn't show off my terrific figure, for example. He's great at getting in a compliment even when he's telling me it's not for me.

Such advice focuses the "wrong" on the external thing rather than on her. Do whatever you can to help her look her best.

Helping the woman you love feel more beautiful will help her want to be more romantic with you.

Activities to Hone Your Romantic Spirit

Following are examples of actions and activities which, according to our survey respondents, express the romantic spirit. Try one or two now, and then come back later for more when you feel comfortable enough to take a few more risks.

- Practice noticing what she does well and tell her that you appreciate her capabilities. Be specific. "The roses look great. You do such a good job in the garden." Then tell her again later. And then next time, choose another capability to praise.
- Take note of what she does for you—from remembering to stop at the store to organizing your socks—and thank her when she does it.

- When among friends or associates, mention something wonderful about your partner: some recent accomplishment or idea, or even something about her that you just recently noticed. Do this in her presence so that she can hear it.
- Practice noticing the way she looks, from when she gets up in the morning to when she goes to bed at night. Keep your antennae up. If she happens to ask, "Why are you looking at me that way?" you can reply, "I'm just noticing how beautiful you are." Or if you're ready, call attention to a detail you haven't verbalized before. And you're on your way to romance.
- What she values in life might be found in how she wants to be remembered. Ask your partner to take part in a little game. Pretend you're both angels, thinking back on your lives. How would you want to be remembered?
- Ask her for advice, and listen to her answers. Let her know that you appreciate her thoughts. Share your ideas with her, as well.

Take Time

When you fell in love, you spent lots of "quality" time with this lovely woman. You listened to her thoughts, hopes, and feelings—all without judging. And you may have bared your own soul, as well. You sought to know her desires, and you accepted, you appreciated, you attempted to fulfill those desires. She felt wanted, needed, and loved. You wanted her to want you, and she did. She eagerly soaked up your sharing, your listening, your attention. And she assumed that it would all continue.

But according to our survey respondents, once a man has his partner's attention, he doesn't feel the need to try as hard to please her. So you see why she might be disappointed? If you no longer spend so much "quality" time with her—sharing, listening, dreaming—then you need to formulate a plan to become the romantic you once were. And if you remember how enjoyable those first days were, you know you'll enjoy this new experience as well.

In his book *Intimate Play*, Dr. William Betcher reminds us that Aristotle once said that "nature requires us not just to work well, but to idle well." Betcher goes on to say:

> My impression is that it's more in the idleness area that couples have trouble. After the initial surge of playfulness has passed, sweeping away schedules and responsibilities, the honeymoon is over and we're back on the assembly line on Monday morning. Unfortunately, the assembly line mentality extends to our lives at home so that we always seem to have time for one more project but not enough to waste. Later we'll have time to enjoy ourselves, we think, after the new addition is finished, after we buy the dishwasher, after the kids get older. Only later never comes.

Play can certainly open up avenues for getting to know each other better—as well as having fun. The woman you love deserves your time. You spend so much time away from her. She wants you to take time to let her know that your relationship is important to you.

Make Her Your Priority

The woman you love wants to feel that she's your first priority, just as you are hers. In your mind, no doubt, she already is Priority One. But she can't read your mind. And just telling her is not enough. *Show* her.

When making plans with others, be sure to consider your partner's needs. If you want to arrange a game of tennis with your friends on Sunday or a round of cards with your buddies on Thursday evening, for example, be sure that you are not compromising your partner's plans or wishes. It's easy enough to tell friends, "I have to check the calendar at home."

And when thinking of how you will spend your available time (your time away from work), include ways that you can spend time with your partner. Make plans with her to do things together on weekends, holidays, and even after work during the week if that's possible. A special night out for dinner during the week can add new spark to your everyday relationship. It doesn't have to happen every Wednesday night, for example, but once in a while. That's what makes it special. Inviting her to spend time with you outside of the time you routinely spend with each other will help her know that she is your priority.

And when you're out with others, make sure you pay particular attention to your partner.

From one of our survey respondents:

> Although we have our special times together, we both feel it is important that we also have our times away from each other with friends or to do as we wish. On Thursday night, he goes out with the guys while I go shopping. And on Sunday morning, he plays tennis while I go to brunch with friends—or with just a good book. But other than these planned times, he always calls me to let me know when he would like to make plans with others. I appreciate that. And I do the same for him. Friday and Saturday nights are sacred—saved for romance.

Make Time for "Us"

Spending time together away from the distractions of others is critical to keeping up a romantic relationship. Two-thirds of women queried rated the statement "He arranges for us to have time alone" as *very important,* yet only one-third told us that it occurs often enough. But when it does, it can be magical:

> During a time when our marriage was frazzled with pre-teen demands, I arrived home from work to find that my husband had come home early and arranged for our twelve-year-old daughter to stay at her friend's place overnight. He had picked up a romantic video that he knew I wanted to see, and he was making dinner— for just the two of us. We had a wonderful night. And it helped put our relationship back on track.

Keep Her in Your Thoughts

Your partner wants to know that you think of her when you're apart—and that you long to be with her. You can satisfy this need by calling her frequently during the week, at her home or place of work. You can leave little notes for her to find after you've left for the day, for the evening, or on a business trip. You can phone her just before you leave work to let her know that you'll be home soon. If she's not home when you call, she'll enjoy coming home to find the message on her answering machine.

And what's the message? Tell her over and over again, in a different way each time: "I'm longing to be with you." "I'm looking forward to seeing you." "I can't wait to hold you again."

If you're going to be late, give her plenty of notice. Unless you're a victim of a natural disaster, if you arrive late without calling ahead, she will feel as if she doesn't matter to you. After all, she was waiting for *you,* looking forward to being with you, maybe even longing for you, so if you walk in late, you can forget about romance. This is one of those "man" habits that drive women away. And if this has been a habit with you, no wonder she's not ready for romance when you finally show up. You've got a lot of making up to do.

As one of our survey respondents reported:

> Listening to some of my women friends, I might think that using a telephone is genetic—only women know how to do it. I'm glad to say that my own husband has somehow acquired the gene.

Keep Her Close

Romance requires closeness. In analyzing responses to our survey, one item stood out above all others: "He touches me with tenderness." Ninety percent of respondents rated it as *very important* but only thirty percent said that men were satisfying them in this area. Under-the-table touches, unexpected hugs, sudden kisses—these are the ways of romance.

Of course it's important that you touch, hug, and kiss your partner prior to, during, and after sex. But it's just as important to let her know that you enjoy being close at all times, by touching, hugging, and kissing her in *nonsexual* ways at times when you are not planning to have sex. Put your hand on hers in a restaurant, touch her face when you're standing close, squeeze her thigh in the car, give her a hug when you part in the morning and when you greet her in the evening. And suddenly you're a romantic.

From one of our survey respondents: "Whenever he's beside me, I can feel it with his touches. His touches let me know that he's glad to be with me. And I'm there for him."

Help Her Be Her Best

Encourage your partner to develop her full potential. Find out her interests and ask her about her dreams. Whether she feels she needs an exercise program, a new résumé, or a better education to fulfill her life's desires, help her find out how to do it. If she needs time, help her make room for it. The more self-worth she gains, the happier her life will be. And the happier you will be to have her by your side.

Activities to Hone Your Romantic Spirit

- Make plans to give "quality" time to your partner—a time when you can play together. Invite her to do something special with you. Maybe it's something you had fun doing while you were dating, maybe it's something you do on occasion now, or maybe it's something new (rent some roller skates at the local rink, take a hike in the woods, sign up for a language course). Make all the preparations (find out when the rink is open, get the map for the hike and maybe even make a picnic, get all the papers needed to sign up for the course).

And follow through. A few weeks later, invite her to do it again—the same activity or something else.

- When making plans to spend time away from your partner, check with her before confirming with others to make sure that your own plans don't interfere with any plans or expectations she had with you.
- Call her frequently—at least a few times a week—just to let her know you're thinking of her. Have something special to say to her each time you call, something as simple as "That was a terrific back rub you gave me this morning," or "I'm looking forward to seeing you this evening."
- If you find you're running late, call her and let her know. Let her know where you are and how late you will be.
- Practice touching her in nonsexual ways. When speaking with her, touch her face, her hair, her hand, her arm. When standing near her, put your hand on her shoulder, or your arm around her waist. When sitting next to her (yes, sit next to her), put your arm around her shoulders, or your hand on her thigh.

Prove Your Love

Like the valiant knight who slays dragons for his princess, you can show your partner that she is your one true love. A woman wants her man to do for her things he has never done for anyone else. This could mean building her a bookcase, writing her love poems, or taking her to Paris. It all depends upon her desires—and your resources.

In his book *Passive Men, Wild Women,* psychiatrist and marriage counselor Pierre Mornell states, "The whole point, it seems to me, of being a hero or heroine, of winning the prize, is to have someone to win for. A loved one with whom to share our success long after the tumult and shouting dies. Someone to offer us lasting applause. That, I think, is what makes the effort worthwhile and complete."

And that is romance.

Lend a Hand

In societies, such as ours, that have developed on the proposition that men bring home the bacon and women cook it, sex roles are stereotyped to the extent that even well-meaning men who do participate in the care of the household have no concept of what their partner is doing to keep home and family together.

When asked "What gets in the way of romance?" our survey respondents listed *time pressures* as the number one "enemy of romance." Moreover, ninety-seven percent of our respondents find it *very important* that their partner be available when they need help.

In spite of the fact that women have shown success in what were once male-dominated realms, such as business, finance, and even warfare, women still hold ultimate responsibility for cooking, shopping, housecleaning, and laundry.

So how can you help? Start by taking on some of the chores. If you're already doing that, take on some more. Even if you don't live in the same household, you have ample opportunity to help her out. If you're handy or have a special skill, you can offer to rewire her stereo, fix her dishwasher, wallpaper her kitchen, or change the oil in her car.

One of our respondents told of her "dream" boyfriend who kept her car gassed, cleaned, and maintained on a regular basis. Another told us that her boyfriend planted a vegetable garden in her backyard—and used it when he came over to cook for her. And a third offered this:

> Shortly after I moved into my first house, I met Arnold. And when he saw my garage, he offered to organize it for me. He brought in shelves and organized everything and swept it out and took loads of stuff to the dump. Finally I could fit my car in! I'll never forget that.

If you're not already in the habit of at least occasionally shopping, preparing meals, and/or cleaning up after meals, try it—she'll like it. If you don't feel creative in the kitchen, you can always pick up carryouts. Even some of the nicer restaurants will pack up a dinner for you—call them and order ahead. Or if you have the means, arrange for a caterer to deliver the dinner.

Offer to vacuum the living room, clean the bathroom, dust the furniture, or take the clothes to the cleaners.

It's important to do this in a way that does not suggest she is not a good housekeeper; she has a busy life and not enough time to do everything.

And of course you never leave your things around for her to pick up.

If you have children, you'll want to read Chapter 6, "If She's a Mom," to learn how to find romance in spite of the diaper pail.

Show Respect

The woman you love wants you to be her hero. No matter how successful she is in her own career, she still needs a man she can look up to. In everything that you do, show her that you are worthy of her love. Any mean-spirited act toward her (or toward anyone whom she cares for) may drive her away. As one respondent wrote, "Constant criticism and unkind remarks will quickly douse any romantic spark."

Anything you do to compromise her in public—from touching her in blatantly sexual ways to verbally putting her down—is sure to kill romance. And remember that "public" includes the family; children will quickly learn who is respectful and who is respected, and they will model their own lives on it. If you don't show respect for Mom, the children won't respect her, either. Any disrespect—in public or private—will only make her feel that *you* are not worthy of her love.

Know your partner, know her tolerances, know her "hot buttons"—what can immediately turn her off. Pay attention to things that frighten her, embarrass her, or anger her. And just don't do them.

Activities to Hone Your Romantic Spirit

- Offer to do something that may be difficult or tedious for her.
- Even if you do not share the same household, you have an opportunity to be the most romantic man she has ever known. Offer to do something helpful. Wash her windows or change the filter on her heater. Then in a week or so, offer to do something else.
- If you have a special talent that could ease her burden, put it to work. This may include anything from changing the oil in her car to planting a tree in her yard.
- Plan an evening at home. Invite her to come home and relax. She can read, bathe, watch TV, or watch you while you take care of everything. Candlelight, music, dinner in a comfortable setting. And be sure to clean up, too. (If, however, you find yourselves swept into the bedroom after dinner, be sure to let her know that you *will* clean up the kitchen the following day.)
- Arrange for meal trade-off. Take turns as "chef" in the kitchen. The "chef" will plan the meal, shop for the groceries, and do the main cooking. The partner will assist in any needed way (for example, peel the potatoes), and clean up afterward. Or share both aspects of the preparation—one of you can make the salad while the other cooks the pasta.
- When she's stressed or busy, protect her. When the doorbell or the phone rings, answer it and, if it's for her, let the caller know that your partner is otherwise occupied. Take a message. Unless it's an emergency, tell all callers she'll get back to them later.
- Do something special for her that you have done for no other woman—build something for her, write something for her, learn something with her, take her somewhere, do something totally wild together. And let her know that you've never done it before.

Know Thy Partner

The most important aspect of romance is to know your own partner—her own desires, wishes, and dreams. But how does a man decipher his woman's mind?

It may not surprise you to learn that the best way to find out what your partner wants is to listen—not only to her words, but also to her actions, her reactions, and the silent words that come between the lines.

One of our survey respondents underlined the importance of this when she shared with us her "date rate" procedure:

> I have this test after a first date. I guess you could call it "who knows more about the other." When I'm back home alone, if I know everything about him and I realize that he knows nothing about me, he's out. And I don't mean that he knows just my favorite restaurant. Did he ask me anything about my hopes and fears, my life goals, my childhood experiences, my ambitions? I don't expect him to know everything on the first date, but I do want to know that he's interested in knowing something about me—the real me.

In order to romance the woman you love, you'll need to find out more about her on a daily basis—not just what she wants for her birthday, but what makes her happy. What makes her sad. What situations make her feel physically or emotionally uncomfortable. What makes her laugh or cry. What are her hopes and dreams. What makes her angry.

Talk Her Talk

Women in general seem to be more perceptive than men are about what people want. Women have a sort of underground communication or extrasensory skill that lets them in on any number of unarticulated feelings. (Your mother was probably your first lesson in this.) And many women assume that men have the same capabilities.

Our survey made this very clear. In answer to the question "Why isn't he more romantic?" survey respondents told us, "He doesn't know what I want."

But isn't this her fault? After all, if she wants something, why doesn't she just say so?

Because it's not romantic, that's why.

Romance is a pretty little drama played out with suspense, intrigue, and surprise. Romance involves working behind the scenes.

Besides, women have been taught that asking for something is rude. If a man cares enough, they say, he'll find out what she wants. In any case, it's much more romantic if it was *his* idea. Well, that's the way many women think.

In her book *You Just Don't Understand: Women and Men in Conversation,* sociolinguist Dr. Deborah Tannen points out the differences—and reasons for the differences—in language between men and women. She describes the two genders as coming from two very different cultures and, because the basis of misunderstandings is so great, she refers to communication between men and women as "cross-cultural" talk. Where women communicate to achieve *intimacy,* men communicate to gain status and achieve *independence.*

In her own studies, Tannen found that women gain intimacy through self-revelation, sharing intimate details with each other and building a network of connections. Knowledge and expertise may be part of a woman's business world, but they are generally not important to those relationships that connect women closely to others, including friendships and love relationships.

Men gain independence through knowledge and expertise, sizing up the competition, negotiating with other men to establish position in the hierarchical order. Providing personal details—particularly details about personal problems—can make a man feel vulnerable among other men. And so a man might wonder why his love partner finds it so surprising that he doesn't know his best friend's plans for the weekend.

"The consequences of these disparate concerns," says Tannen, is "very different ways of speaking." It also means very different ways of listening.

Hear Her

In his book *Men Are from Mars, Women Are from Venus,* Dr. John Gray sheds another light on the topic. "Just as women are sensitive to feeling rejected when they don't get the attention they need, men are sensitive to feeling that they have failed when a woman talks about problems. This is why it is so hard for him to listen sometimes. He wants to be the hero. When *she* is disappointed or unhappy over anything, *he* feels like a failure. Her unhappiness confirms his deepest fear: he is just not good enough."

The fact is, women *don't* need men to solve all their problems. If a man tries to quickly solve her problem, it may only diminish the importance of the problem and invalidate the woman's feelings. Mostly, women want men to listen, to understand, to appreciate their situation—like a good therapist. Know this and you'll feel much freer when your partner asks for your support. Instead of trying to come up with an answer, hold her, comfort her. Thank her for sharing her thoughts with you. Let her know that you're there to support her.

According to Dr. M. Scott Peck,

True listening, total concentration on the other, is always a manifestation of love. An essential part of true listening is the discipline of bracketing, the temporary giving up or setting aside of one's own prejudices, frames of reference and desires so as to experience as far as possible the speaker's world from the inside, stepping inside his or her shoes. This unification of speaker and listener is actually an extension and enlargement of ourselves, and new knowledge is always gained from this. Moreover, since true listening involves bracketing, a setting aside of the self, it also temporarily involves a total acceptance of the other. Sensing this acceptance, the speaker will feel less and less vulnerable and more and more inclined to open up the inner recesses of his or her mind to the listener. As this happens, speaker and listener begin to appreciate each other more and more, and the duet dance of love is again begun.

And Peck later goes on to say, "Couples are often surprised, even horrified, when we suggest to them that among the things they should do is talk to each other by appointment. It seems rigid and unromantic and unspontaneous to them. Yet true listening can occur only when time is set aside for it and conditions are supportive of it. It cannot occur when people are driving, or cooking or tired and anxious to sleep or easily interrupted or in a hurry."

Your partner wants you to not only listen, but to *hear* her. She wants you to pay attention to her concerns. If you're used to coming home complaining, expecting her to boost your emotions and self-esteem, try playing her part for a while. Ask her about her day, about what went wrong as well as what went right. You don't have to fix it for her, just listen and sympathize. Give her a hug. Tell her you appreciate her situation. Ask her questions to bring out more details. Help her come to some sort of resolution—without trying to solve her problems for her.

One survey respondent wrote:

> What's romantic for me? Someone who would go on long walks with me, who would have long conversations with me, who would be intelligent and thoughtful and who wouldn't expect that the evening would necessarily culminate in sex. Low lights? Candles? Footsie? Give me a break! I want to be with someone I can trust, someone who is attentive to what I have to say.

If she calls you at work, be prepared to listen and support her. If she calls you at an inconvenient time, do not put her off with a quick answer; instead, let her know that you are in the middle of something that keeps you from giving her your full attention, and schedule another time (within an hour, if possible) to call her back and discuss the situation. Allow at least half an hour (you'd do the same for a colleague who had a concern to discuss). If you have an office door, close it while you're on the phone with your partner.

Share Your Thoughts and Feelings

Less than half the women surveyed felt that their partners give emotionally as much as they themselves do, although over eighty percent felt that it's *very important* that their partners do so.

Women have traditionally been disappointed in men's silence at home. Although men have a lot to say in public, at home they're prone to silence. In *You Just Don't Understand: Women and Men in Conversation,* author Deborah Tannen shares some insight into this aspect of the home relationship. Where women's talk is for interaction, she says, men's talk is for information. For a woman, "listening is a way to show interest and caring"; for a man, it is a way to get information.

So what does all that mean for romance? If you want her to respond to you, listen to her on her terms. Look at the art of conversation from her point of view: she wants to be intimate with you. To do so, she will ask you details of your day, of your life—and she wants you to ask about hers.

She has probably been trying to tell you what she wants in many little ways, but unless you've been actively listening, you haven't heard them.

Acknowledge her day, her person, her conversation. Move a little in her direction, and she'll move a little in yours. And that's when you start "hearing" those desires that she doesn't actually articulate. And the more you know about her, the more chance you have of pleasing her.

Let Her Help

A woman in love wants to support her partner. If you have difficulties at work, a concern about friends or family, a painful situation that makes you want to escape, then by all means share it with the woman you love. She will feel special if you allow yourself to be vulnerable with her. And she will respect you for your honesty. Even if she doesn't have all the answers, she can provide support, comfort, and nurturing.

Activities to Hone Your Romantic Spirit

- Pay attention to nonverbal clues that may indicate your partner's mood, her reaction to things that you do and her reaction to her own experiences. Confirm what you see by asking her: "You seem upset. Tell me about it." "You seem particularly happy tonight. Let me in on it." Don't let her shrug it off. Probe for details: "Tell me more."
- Talk with your partner about her lifelong dreams. Encourage her to attain those dreams. Note anything that you can do to help her.
- When she calls for your attention, put down the paper, mute the TV, look up and listen. Think about what she is saying. Repeat it if you don't understand (i.e., "You're telling me that . . ."). Then comment on it. And wait and listen for her reaction to your comment.
- Set an appointment to talk with your partner—just talk— with minimal distractions. It could be at home, in a restaurant over a meal or coffee, or on a hike in the woods. If the appointment is to take place at home, make sure it is at a time when children and others are away. Sit down together, turn off phones, and be prepared to not answer the door. Make this a regular part of your weekly schedule.
- Read Deborah Tannen's book, *You Just Don't Understand: Women and Men in Conversation,* and John Gray's book, *Men Are from Mars, Women Are from Venus.* Share what you learn with your partner.

3

Romance Every Day

We can all imagine the grand romantic moments: the passionate embrace for the returning hero, the starlight dance on the deck of a cruise ship, the dinner for two by a campfire on a mountain peak. You've seen them in movies, and you may have even experienced similar events yourself. Such grand moments can certainly be very romantic, but lasting romance exists in a continuum of smaller things that you and your partner do to please each other on a regular basis.

When love is in first bloom, romance is fun and easy. You are both on your best, willing to pay loads of attention to each other just to please and be pleased. Later, however, as you greet each other every day—and not always at your best—you may find that the romantic bloom is buried under the snow of daily maintenance. To be sure, long-term relationships that have matured with love offer many compensating qualities, including trust, mutual acceptance, and companionship; and it is unreasonable to expect the early excitement to return. But there are many ways that you can break through the daily grind and reach toward a new kind of romance.

In fact, opportunities exist all around you—opportunities for you to spontaneously "romance" your partner. Unfortunately, such opportunities all too often pass unnoticed. How can you prepare in advance to take advantage of these opportunities?

Today, for the sake of convenience and efficiency, we've isolated ourselves from other people. Instead of the traditional bank teller, we're offered the ATM; instead of the customer service representative on the other end of the phone line, we're faced with a recording; and instead of the personal business meeting, we have E-Mail, voice mail, and video conferences. These are all time-saving, money-saving, and efficient, to be sure. But nobody's really there for you. These impersonal methods of communication only increase the need for personal attention at home. The bottom line for you, the romantic, is to let that woman you love know that *you* are there for *her.*

As one of our survey respondents told us:

> What is romance? Well, after being out in the world all day where nobody seems to care, it's so comfortable to come home to Brian. He's always got a hug for me and wants to hear about my day. For me, that's romance.

With every moment you are with her, you have an opportunity either to *enhance* the relationship or to *not enhance* the relationship. Your choice.

In writing the first draft of this book, we shared the manuscript with a number of male reviewers. One of our reviewers told us that if every man read this chapter, the world would be a much happier place.

Here we ask *you* to take the lead. Based upon what women have told us they want, we offer many activities for you to try. *But don't think you have to try them all.* (The list itself will overwhelm you.)

For starters, choose one romantic action you can practice on a regular basis, something that's comfortable for you. For example, if you're not already in the habit of greeting her whenever she arrives at the door, begin now. Then let the sound that precedes her arrival—the sound of the car in the street, the garage door closing, the footsteps on the walk—be a reminder. Get up and go to her. Then start associating all doors with romance (open the car door for her, think of her as you close your office door and give her a call, give her a hug as you approach your mother's door together, hold her arm as you leave through the church door). And you will suddenly think of romance—spontaneously—whenever you see a door. Pretty easy, actually. Once you've got that one down, you're ready to add something else to your romantic repertoire.

Soon you'll be thinking of all sorts of possibilities every time you're with your lady, as well as when you're away from her You're suddenly a spontaneous romantic—having fun pleasing her—and reaping additional rewards that are sure to come as she pleases you back. Now you've got the romantic spirit.

Your romantic attitude will lead to a more open, more communicative, and deeper relationship in which you learn of each other's needs and desires. And that can only lead to a better way of relating in general. She'll begin to be more romantic as well, anxious to serve *your* needs and desires.

"When Carl shows me that he's there for me," wrote one survey respondent, "I'm there for him as well."

Capture the Moment

No matter who you are or what your relationship, you can capture the moment and make it romantic. Take a look at the suggestions that follow and try as many as are comfortable. Make them a permanent part of your relationship. Then reach out and try a few more. Pace yourself. Let her see your romantic spirit unfold. And then when you're ready, challenge yourself—take a risk. And watch romance blossom.

Touch Her

As mentioned earlier, women told us again and again that they do not get enough touching. Hold her arm or her hand when you walk with her. Put your arm around her. Touch her shoulder or her elbow when coming across the room to greet her.

If you're not in the habit of touching outside of the bedroom—or if you haven't touched her in a nonsexual way in a while—then start right now. Touch her hair and say it's soft and it smells so good. Touch her blouse and tell her that the color is great on her. Touch her hand across the dinner table.

When watching a film or theater performance, put your arm around her shoulders or clasp your hand around hers. After you seat her in a restaurant, stand behind her for a moment and gently touch her shoulders.

When conversing with her, touch her cheek, her hair, and smile into her eyes.

This little change in your way of relating can dramatically affect your relationship.

Many of our survey respondents told us of the importance of touching. Here's one example:

> I hadn't known Glen very long when he invited me over to his place for a video and popcorn. Soon after I arrived, he went to his bedroom and, when he came out, he was rubbing hand lotion into his hands. He came close to me and said he had too much lotion and took my hands and shared the lotion with me, giving me a wonderful hand massage. He was the most sensual guy I had ever met. And now that we're living together, I've become much more aware of my own sensuality—as well as his.

The act of touching in a nonthreatening way—just taking her arm as you walk down the sidewalk, for example—will start the romantic feelings flowing.

Again and again, women told us that they find sensual stimuli oh-so-romantic—sensuality not necessarily for sex, but for its own luscious enjoyment. And women just don't get enough touching. Use stroking instead of grabbing. Massage her shoulders. Stroke her hair. Touch gently. Walk your fingers across her back. Brush your body against her skin. This heightened sensual closeness can only lead to greater intimacy. Women want it.

Greet Her

Greet her whenever you've been apart from each other for more than a few hours. This does not mean yelling up the stairs, "Hi Honey, I'm home," etc. It's important that you create your own greeting style, based upon your mutual desires. The greeting can include touching, maybe kissing, and a personal hello.

If you don't already practice hugging, start now. Whenever you come home to her or whenever she comes home to you, from an extended business trip or a walk around the block with the dog, give her a hug. A quick squeeze or a big bear hug—make hugging a habit.

According to a recent article in *The Wall Street Journal* titled "People Are Hugging a Lot More Now and Seem to Like It":

> Hugging obviously is good for you. Parents and children know that Lovers do, too. It's safe sex. Researchers say touch in general reduces anxiety, increases self-esteem and provides a connection for newborns, whose senses are developing, and for the elderly, whose senses are waning. Hugging, a firm form of touch, stimulates the nervous system. Without touch, researchers say, the organism doesn't thrive and may not survive. Studies of orphanages have proved that.

Once regular hugging becomes natural to you, you might add a kiss—sometimes light, sometimes thick and sexy.

Finally, tell her that you've missed her, that you're so glad to be back with her.

Pay attention to your voice when it greets her. Try listening to your voice on a tape recorder. Does it sound happy to see her? If not, practice. Think of her as someone you want to please, impress, fascinate. And you will.

As you greet her with a hug, a kiss, and a personal hello, try to get in touch with that brief second of electrical current that pulsates between you. If it isn't there, make it happen. Practice it. Send her the current and feel what she gives back. Prolong it.

Try this: Before you greet her, smile to yourself about the fact that you're about to see the one you love. Think of the best times with her. Close your eyes for a few moments, relax, let the day fall away from your shoulders. Then open the door and *voila!* You're looking good.

One of our survey respondents told us of her pleasure in the way her husband greets her:

> When he comes home he sometimes pretends he's been away for months trekking through the rain forest or lost in an avalanche—even when he's just come in from taking out the garbage. And he gives me what he calls his "survivor's" hug. And oh! I do welcome him home.

Surprise Her

Women love surprises.

Go ahead and send her roses on Valentine's Day, but also send flowers on other days for no reason other than to say "I want to please you." Because that's what flowers say.

If you keep a calendar, you can pencil in the word "surprise" once a week or once a month or as often as you wish. This week on a Tuesday, next week on a Friday, and so on. Maybe this week it's flowers and next week it's a little love note and three weeks later an invitation for a night on the town and next month . . . well, you get the picture. Not a habit of a certain *activity,* but a habit of *surprise.* Keep her guessing . . . keep her interested.

Be sure to take a look at Chapter 7, "Occasions, Gifts, and Such," for ideas on surprising her for no special reason.

By giving her surprises on a regular basis, you will develop a more spontaneous attitude toward life. And this will help you to take advantage of opportunities as they arise. Here is an example provided by one of our survey respondents:

We had been dating for about a month, though I wasn't keeping track. I arrived home to find in my mailbox a love poem entitled "The First Month with the Woman I Love." Today he continues to surprise me—when I least expect it: roses on my pillow, special dinners waiting for me when I arrive home, coupons for "the chore of the day" on Saturday mornings. I would do anything for him.

Activities to Hone Your Romantic Spirit

Following are examples of actions and activities which, according to our survey respondents, express the romantic spirit. Try one or two now, and then come back later for more when you feel comfortable enough to take a few more risks.

- When you arrive home, seek her out and kiss her. When she comes through the door, go to greet her. Tell her how wonderful she looks, feels, and smells. Do this as often as possible.
- Touch her at least once every day you're with her. Hold her hand. Touch her when you're talking with her—even if it's just talking about the laundry. Touch her hand when sitting next to her or across from her at the dining room table. Hold her arm when you go out together. Put your arm around her waist or her shoulder. Show her that you want her there with you.
- When she's in the middle of a project (making dinner, doing taxes, working overtime), come up behind her and rub her shoulders or give her a great big hug.
- Mark your calendar with reminders to surprise her. And start a list of little things you can do to surprise her.

Communicate

The previous chapter, "Women's Romantic Desires," discussed differences in communication styles between men and women.

Keeping this in mind, it's important to practice meaningful communication with your partner every day that you are together.

To help her feel that you are truly communicating with each other, be open to receiving. When she wants to talk, listen—even when she wants to complain. She'll feel much better after she's said what she wants to say. Don't argue with her. Let her just run it out. Then go to her and hug her. Acknowledge her feelings (even if she's been complaining about you). And watch her melt.

Just as important, express your own feelings to her. Don't worry about appearing weak or stupid. Women have told us that their partners don't share enough with them. Your own partner will be delighted that you trust your feelings with her. Even if you're upset with her, let her know—calmly. Don't let resentment build up any longer.

Ask her questions that are open-ended rather than those that can be answered with a "yes" or "no." Instead of "Did you have a good day?" try "Tell me about your day" or "You seem a bit upset . . . what's going on?"

And be sure to keep up with *her* interests so that you can discuss them with her.

Call Her

If you keep a calendar, write her name on it in a few places each week, and call her—from the office, from the golf course, from the business trip to New Jersey. Just to say that you're thinking of her. Let her know about your day. Ask her about *her* day. That's all. Just call her. Schedule it in the way that you would schedule a meeting. But instead of making a habit of it—i.e., every Monday morning at 10—try 3 PM on Monday and then 10 AM on Thursday and the following week 9 AM on Tuesday and, well, you get it. Mix it up. Instead of becoming just another routine responsibility, the calls become a surprise.

Incidentally, when she calls you, listen to what she has to say without judging her words or coming up with solutions to her problems. Support her ideas and feelings. And before you hang up, let her know that *you* were thinking of *her.* "I was about to call you . . ." is certainly appropriate. Because of course you were.

Keep your own conversation short. Make her want more. Practice ending conversations graciously. It doesn't have to be "I'm busy" or "I'd better get back to my work now" because that only makes her feel that she isn't as important as whatever it is that you're doing. Instead, say something such as "I can't wait to see you later. Bye for now." Or "I'd better hang up or I'll have to come see you right now." Or "The sooner I get this done, the faster I'll be in your arms." Corny? Well, that depends upon your relationship. Find what works best for you.

Compliment Her

Women love compliments. Not frivolous and transparent flattering words, but compliments of substance. She's heard plenty of ordinary compliments about the way she looks—compliments that are quickly dismissed as "rote" or "lines." Let her know that you see the specialness in her—her individuality.

Be constantly on the lookout for reasons to compliment her—observe what she does, what she says, how she looks, whatever. By doing this you will not only please her, but you will also build her confidence and self-esteem, and her positive qualities will grow. If she has to fish for compliments, it may mean that you haven't been paying attention.

Notice what she wears, how she smells, how she moves. Give her details—not just "Oh you look great tonight," but "That skirt shows off just enough to keep me watching all evening . . ." Also compliment her on her accomplishments. Notice the small things and celebrate the large ones—from the closet she organized to the promotion she received at the office.

What this all means is that you've got to pay close attention to your partner. And that in itself adds to your romantic spirit.

She'll feel more beautiful, sexier, excited, if you let her know that you notice how terrific she really is. If you want to be Number One in her life, make her Number One in yours.

Surprise her. Give her compliments when she least expects them, not just when she's all dressed up to go out with you, but during the most ordinary times—at the dinner table, as she's folding the laundry, when she emerges from the shower, as she reads to your child.

Tell her you enjoy her company. You're glad that she was with you to share this evening or afternoon or weekend. And you're looking forward to sharing more time with her.

Let her know that she is special to you.

Show Appreciation

When she does something for you—special or otherwise—let her know that you not only appreciate what she has done but that you also appreciate *her.* After she's prepared a meal for you (even if you don't like the particular dish), let her know that you appreciate all the time she spent shopping, preparing, and serving it. Start by telling her. Maybe add a touch, a hug, a kiss. Make a habit of it.

Likewise, show appreciation for other "chores" she may be performing for you. Thank her for going to the grocery store, for picking up your socks, for taking little Suzie to gymnastics class. Find something—no matter how small—each day, and thank her. Tell her once and then tell her again. For a special touch, put it into writing (refer to Chapter 5, "Love Notes").

Show appreciation for her *ideas,* as well. Be sure to give her credit and let her know that you appreciate her creativity when she comes up with ideas and suggestions for your home, business, or plans for the future.

Show Her You're with Her

Say her name with love behind it . . . she wants to hear her name.

After attending a performance (a film, a symphony, a lecture), discuss it with her. Elicit *her* ideas—or her feelings or her fears and dreams. And when she surprises you with new thoughts and feelings, let her know that you want to know her better—even if you think you already do. Yes, if you give her a chance, she just may surprise *you*.

When in a gathering of your friends or associates, introduce her as if you're pleased that she's with you. One respondent was pleased to tell us that her husband introduces her as "my wife and best friend."

And while you're mingling, don't mingle too far. Too often partners go their separate ways, coming together again only when the carriage is about to turn into a pumpkin. Sure, take off to find your good buddies, but come back again and again to remind her that you're glad she came with you. From one of our respondents:

Bruce and I have always loved parties. And throughout our relationship, every time we go to a party, even though he and I go our separate ways to talk with friends, he comes back every once in a while to kiss me or put his hand on my arm or my shoulder or refill my glass. If nothing else, he catches my eye and winks or blows me a kiss. He says he's so proud to be with me.

And from another:

We were in the crowded elevator on the way up to the auditorium where he was to give a lecture when he put his arm around my shoulder and leaned over and whispered in my ear that he would be watching my eyes all through his presentation because I gave him the confidence that he needed.

Tell Her

Unless you tell her regularly that you love her, no matter how many times you may have said it in the past—unless you tell her now, today, she will think that you don't. So tell her. You have absolutely nothing to lose. She'll love you back. And how bad is that?

Whisper to her—in the kitchen, in the hallway, at a party. Sweet little nothings such as "I can't wait to be alone with you," "You keep me wanting you," or just "Oh Sally" (if that's her name, of course . . .).

Write to her. Yes, even if you live under the same roof. Write her a love letter. And watch her smile.

Activities to Hone Your Romantic Spirit

- Whenever you notice how lovely she is (when her hair shines in the light or when she smiles in that beautiful way), tell her. Tell her you love to smell her hair or see her smile or watch her eyes sparkle when she laughs.
- Start to open up the lines of communication. Ask her what she *thinks* about something. Ask her how she *feels* about something. Ask her about her *dreams, desires, expectations.*
- Mark your calendar with reminders to call her.
- Do something special for her this week to let her know that your relationship is important to you—she's important to you—and you want to please her.
- Write her a little note telling her you love her and you're anxious to be with her. Put it in a special place where she'll find it when you're not home (in her lingerie drawer, on her dashboard, in the mail, in a kitchen pot . . .).
- Make up a loving and attractive nickname for her. Test it with her and see how she responds. If it works, begin to use it in intimate ways.

Create Quality Time

The term "quality time" has long been associated with the need for parents to spend a certain amount of time with their children, doing things that focus on the children's growth and happiness: open discussions at the dinner table or afternoons at the ball park, for example. In other words, spending time beyond the bare essentials of feeding and clothing a youngster.

You and your partner need "quality time" together as well—time that will enhance the quality and growth of *your* relationship. Unless you already spend a fair share of your time pursuing activities together that you both enjoy, this may take some planning.

Most of our survey respondents wrote that they feel a need to spend more time with their partner in order to keep their relationship strong.

How do you spend your time together?

Share Nature

Share small natural delights together. They're all around you, just waiting for you to take advantage of them. Sunrises and sunsets, the moon and the stars, the smell of rain and the crackle of fire. The tiny flowers deep in the woods. The singing birds. The storms. The warmth of the afternoon sun. You might want to start an outdoor awareness program and share your feelings about the beauty of nature with your partner. These natural, sensual delights serve to add romance when they are shared.

Walking hand-in-hand together in the outdoors, in fact, was a common romantic element mentioned by our respondents. Inclement weather can add to the romance, whether you enjoy it in front of a fireplace or out in the storm. As one of our survey respondents reported:

It was pouring rain, and our dog needed a walk. John and I traded looks about who was going to take him and we each tried to busy ourselves with something else. "Ok," John finally said to me as Buster whined at the door. "I'll go if you go." So we put on our rain gear and went out for one of the most delightful evenings. We chased puddles and splashed each other. When we arrived back home, John made a fire and we toweled each other dry and spent cozy hours in front of the fireplace. Romantic? Yes!

Develop Common Interests

It's imperative that you each have your own interests outside the relationship, lest one or both of you depend too much on the other for excitement and stimulation. You want to continue to grow and learn and bring new ideas and experiences back to each other. Otherwise, you may feel as if you're talking to yourself! But also explore what you might enjoy in common— whether it's going dancing or climbing mountains. You'll be amazed how a simple thing like a stroll around the block together a few times a week will bring your partner closer and add to the romance of your relationship.

With a little planning, you can "grow" your time together. Think about how you spend your time (work, leisure activities, home maintenance, whatever) and take a moment to compare the time you spend on each of these activities with the importance you would like it to have in your life. If you want to become a more romantic guy, you're going to have to give a higher priority to your love relationship. Depending upon the current state of your relationship, this may mean giving up time in another area for time on romance. Just as important, however, is *how* you spend that time.

Maybe there's something you used to do together when you first met: jogging, fishing, playing chess, whatever. Would your partner enjoy getting back into it?

Or maybe it's best for you to find something new, which you're both interested in exploring together. Learning a new skill together brings its own excitement and rewards.

Find out if your partner wants to take tennis lessons or gourmet cooking lessons or dance lessons, and then check out your community services to see what's available. Look into clubs and organizations in your area. Do you like to ski, practice yoga, run marathons? Maybe there's a group you can join. Bowling anyone? Pull out the Yellow Pages and look up gyms and health clubs where you can swim or work out on a regular basis. How about parks—places where you can hike or picnic or ride a bike.

Know what she likes to do, how she would choose to spend her free time. One survey respondent wrote: "It would mean so much to me if he would participate in something in which he has no vested interest, just to do it for me."

And from another respondent:

Doug bought me a pair of roller blades for my birthday—and one for himself as well. I'm a new person now. I'm getting into great shape. And we're having so much fun together.

And yet another.

Joey and I saved for years for that big trip to Italy. Once we knew it was a reality, he went to the bookstore and bought language tapes. And every night we listened and learned. Over there, we practiced the language. And now that we're back home, we're still speaking Italian together—even when we're in a crowd. It's like making love in public. And it reminds us of what a terrific time we had over there. Next stop: France.

What does *she* like to do? Ask her or surprise her—but whatever you do, get out there with her and have fun.

Provide Special Treatment

When a woman is not feeling her best, she might like a little extra care. Survey respondents wrote that they appreciated special treatment when they were not feeling well. One example:

I hadn't been dating Jeffrey for all that long, and I frankly didn't know if I was serious about him. When I got the flu, I not only felt terrible physically, but I felt so guilty that I had to break a very special date he had planned for us—to see the *Nutcracker* ballet. But he was good about it. That night he came over to check on me and brought along the video *Lady and the Tramp,* remembering that I had said I always had wanted to see it. He was so sweet and thoughtful that night even though I looked and felt a mess. Anyone who can accept me in that state and actually want to be with me, well, I knew he was the man for me. Now we've been happily married for five years.

Get Away

Besides time spent together on a regular basis, vacations are also important.

Women generally take primary responsibility for the care of their home. And no matter how much your partner loves her domicile, when she's at home, she's forever thinking of "chores." So take her away.

"Time away alone with partner" scored in the top ten romantic preferences among our survey respondents, especially among married women.

Go somewhere you've never been before. It can bring an entirely new perspective to your relationship. It doesn't have to be expensive or exotic. But whether it's white-river rafting, a long weekend in the city, or a trip to Tahiti, make sure it's something you *both* enjoy (if she doesn't play tennis, don't vacation at a tennis resort—unless of course she wants to learn).

If you're both exhausted from the daily grind, however, planning an action-packed vacation might be too much like work. Just sitting back and doing nothing might be what your relationship really needs. Try taking a mini-vacation at home. Turn off the phone. Send the kids to the sitter. Take a walk together, share the newspaper on the back porch, take a trip to the grocery with her and make dinner together, rent a video, make popcorn. Have fun.

Activities to Hone Your Romantic Spirit

- Write a schedule of how you spend your time. Are you giving enough "quality time" to your relationship? If not, seriously consider cutting back on time spent on things that aren't as important as your relationship. Take an afternoon off once in a while to take your partner shopping, take a morning off to laze a bit longer in bed and then go out to brunch together, or take off a Monday or Friday and plan something special for a long weekend.

- If your partner does not have activities she enjoys outside the relationship, encourage her to get involved in a sport, club, or exercise.

- If you don't have a common activity that you pursue on a regular basis, discuss this with your partner and make a list of some activities you might want to try together. Develop an action plan. Take responsibility for following through by checking out fitness centers, bridge clubs, community classes, or whatever it is that needs to be investigated.

- Watch the newspaper for coming attractions in your area or in the nearest city. There's always an opportunity to experience a new event, whether it's the county fair or the Bolshoi Ballet. Take advantage of local opportunities and experience them together.

- If she needs "time out," help her find it. Take care of business for her so that she can take off for a few hours or a few days. And she'll come back refreshed and appreciative.

- Begin to plan that vacation you both dream of. Start a "Vacation Only" savings account to pay for it. Visit a travel agent to learn about things to do, places to stay, and alternatives for getting there. If the dream vacation is years away, find out about inexpensive romantic spots nearby for interim trysts.

- Take a walk under the stars and share your feelings.

Court Her

When a man is dating a woman, he pays special attention to her. He calls her. He sends her flowers. He tells her how lovely she is. He might even overextend himself financially to please her. He does everything he can to make sure that when she thinks of romance, she thinks of him.

Even if you've been with her for years, it's time you started dating her. The whole idea of a "date" can bring new excitement to your relationship.

In her book *The Erotic Silence of the American Wife*, Dalma Heyn points out the need for excitement in a relationship—and the adultery that can occur when it isn't there. A woman seeks excitement outside marriage when her own man doesn't think that excitement is important at home.

When carried out in a romantic spirit, dating your partner can create the romantic tension that will have her wanting to be in *your* arms.

Flirt with Her

Romance is more fun when it's just a little naughty. Naughtiness adds excitement, interest, intrigue. And flirting helps create that naughty mood.

In flirting, attitude is everything. Smile to yourself. Put a wink in your eye. Picture yourself as Don Juan and your woman as that elusive one you've been after for so long. Remember the singles scenes when you wanted to attract someone new? Well, your partner is worth at least that much attention. Here she comes, and you've got about three minutes to win her over before she's off to dance with someone else. Exercise whatever flirting skills you used in the past. And read on to gain some new ones.

If flirting is new to your relationship, your partner may not be ready to respond as you might imagine just yet. She may touch your forehead, ask if you have a fever. Flirting requires patience, subtlety, confidence. If she responds with "Not tonight, I've got a headache," that only means that in the past you've done this just for sex. No no no. This is just for fun. So smile and take it in and keep it up. Soon enough she'll be playing the game. (On the other hand, if she's not used to this fun from you, be prepared to drop everything and follow her quick step up to the bedroom.)

Flirting can be risky. What if I'm rejected? Don't worry, if it doesn't work today, try it again tomorrow. Life's too short to shortchange your romance.

One of our respondents told us about her spontaneous flirtatious man. In response to the question "Tell us about a romantic experience," she responded:

> Things hadn't been going so well. We hadn't had sex in ages. And then one night as we were making dinner, one of our favorite songs came on the radio. He took my hand out of the salad bowl and danced me across the kitchen floor. I was surprised and thrilled . . . and I knew there was hope for us yet.

Be a kid again and bring out the child in her:

> Sometimes he pretends it's our first date, and he acts as if he's come to pick me up and my parents just left us alone for a few hours and he wants to make the most of it. We have so much fun.

Make contact with her eyes. And smile when you do it.

Use her name—again and again, or use her pet name. A pet name is an intimate "insider" communication. (If you don't have a pet name for her, find one that seems sweet and natural for her, something sexy and personal that only the two of you would understand—a name that makes her smile.)

From one respondent:

> It doesn't have to be words. Sometimes he gives me that low-pitched growl or that "ummmm" with the somnolent look that tells me that he finds me so so attractive. Ei yi yi!

Give her a double take from across the room. How's that? Try a quick glance her way, then a glance away, and then a slooooow comeback. As if you want to return to something you almost missed. Smile your sexiest, slyest, most sensuous smile as you capture her in that last slow look.

Whisper in her ear. Even the most mundane statements take on romantic connotations if whispered: "Let's adjourn to the living room." "How about chicken for dinner." "You've got sauce on your lip."

Whispering connotes a special, intimate connection. Even "I'll take out the garbage now," when whispered, can sound pretty sexy. And a kiss on the neck, a tongue in the ear, or a slow sweep of your fingers through her hair adds flair to the flirting.

Move toward her with your best flirting smile and eye contact. Hold that gaze just a bit longer than she might expect. Back off quickly, suddenly preoccupied. Then come back slowly, smiling, whispering, touching. Wow! She'll be waiting for more. This can happen all within a few minutes, or it can happen within a few hours—flirt with her when you arrive home, then go change your clothes or start up the barbecue or watch the news and then come back with that great flirting style again.

Take charge of the atmosphere. Choose the music, the lighting, the room. Bring pillows to the couch and food and drink to the living room table. Turn off the TV. Turn off the phone. Serve her. Invite her to sit with you and cuddle. Create your own intimate atmosphere, free from distraction.

Show your hand. Palmists will tell you that people who hide their palms and wrists are not open. People who show their palms and separate their fingers are willing to open up to those around them. Putting your open hand, palm up, out toward someone—on a table, for example—invites the other to become intimate. Try it.

Take Her Out

When you take her on a date, where do you go? What do you do? Is it something that your partner wants to do? Do you even know what she wants to do? Well if you want to be romantic, it's time you found out. Start by asking her.

You might take a look at your local newspaper for coming events and ask her what she thinks about going to a play or a symphony or a basketball game. Look at the restaurant column and ask her if she's interested in trying a new spot. Dinner dates at candlelit restaurants were especially popular among survey respondents.

It's not where you go for the date that's important of course; it's that you're spending special time together. Keep in mind that variety—in your approach as well as in your choice of activities—helps keep a romantic spot in the relationship. Even the way in which you invite her can add spice and excitement. Maybe this week it's a call from your office; next week it's a sexy invitation on her answering machine; and later, a written invitation to a special event.

To enhance the romance of the event, be sure to do it right. Days before the date, make a point of complimenting her charms. This helps build the excitement. This helps set the mood. Remember, romance is cumulative.

Prepare yourself for the date. Even if you've been married for years, think back on those courting days and remember how you spent time grooming so that she would be attracted to you. Shower, shave, put on cologne if she likes it. Wear fresh clean clothes, her favorite shirt, the tie she bought you. Polish your shoes, brush your teeth.

And when she does the same, be sure to take time to inhale the fresh scent of her hair and tell her how pleased you are that she is your date for the evening.

For some women, even one insensitive comment could ruin an incredibly romantic mood. Know her "hot buttons": "What's that thing on your face?" "What did you do to your hair!" "Are you going to wear that thing tonight!" Keep it to yourself. A warm encouraging "Baby, you look hot tonight!" will do just fine.

Mind your manners. On the way out the front door, help her into her coat. Hold her arm as you guide her toward the car or the bus or the train station. (If it's cold or stormy, warm up the car for her and then bring it to a place where she can easily get in.) Open her car door *first* (if she's used to opening it herself, say "Let me get that for you") and wait until she gets in and gets cozy until you close it. Then go around and open yours.

Take her arm when walking down the sidewalk or up the stairs. Open the door to the restaurant or the theater or the friend's house and follow her in. Pull out her chair when she sits at the table. And if you want to really impress her when you're sitting at a dinner table, stand up whenever she does, and when she returns to the table, stand up again until she is seated. For an added flair, pull out her chair as she comes to the table so that you can push it in again once she's seated. If she's not used to this behavior, she'll probably think you've flipped—but of course she'll love it.

After you receive your drinks, toast her. Look into her eyes (not at the glass) and tell her how glad you are that she is with you. Even something as simple as "To us!" will make her smile.

Such manners do not imply that your partner is incapable of taking care of herself. Instead, good manners are a sign of respect. You care about her. You want to please her. You anticipate her needs and desires.

The same is true for money matters.

Consider this paragraph from Emily Post's *Etiquette,* dated 1945:

> In this modern day, when women are competing with men in politics, in business and in every profession, it is really senseless to cling to that one obsolete convention—no matter what the circumstances—that the man must buy the tickets, pay the check, pay the taxi, or else be branded a gigolo or a parasite.

Of course this is even truer today. Women have clearly demonstrated their capability to support themselves. And if you and your partner have been together for a while, you've probably already sorted out who pays for what. But even if you do share expenses, your special "dates"—the ones for which you invite her—will be much more romantic if *you* take care of the bills, without any comment on how costly your evening may have been. If she offers to pay her share, let her know that she can ask *you* out for a date some time soon.

> Back before I met Greg, when I was still dating around, I had my own private "code of ethics," I guess you'd call it. If I decided on a first date that I didn't want to see this guy again, I'd insist on paying my share so that I wouldn't feel guilty about saying no if he asked me out again. But if I did want to see someone again, I sat back and let him pay the entire bill; that way I had a wonderful excuse to call him up and invite *him* out usually to my place for dinner.

On the way home, drive somewhere romantic and share the night air and scenery. (Remember how to "make out" in the car?) When you return home, kiss her at the doorstep and ask if you can come in for a nightcap—yes, even if you share the same address. Read the signals. You knew how to do it back then. So what if the neighbors spy—they're only jealous.

Relive the Good Times

If you've been in a long-term relationship, think about those early times. Remember how you met? What were you doing? What were you wearing? How did you approach her, or how did you react when she approached you? In what way did you flirt and let her know that you were interested? What was it that drew her to you? What did you talk about? Try courting her the way you did back then, and maybe she'll react the way she once did.

You probably acted more playful with each other back then. Teasing, touching, laughing at things that weren't even funny, just because you were so happy. And in the early days of your relationship, even washing the car or cleaning the garage together was fun—as you got suds all over each other or stopped in the middle of folding a box to sneak a kiss. Whatever it was, you *played* more in the early courting days than you do now. You had so much fun that you only needed to be in each other's presence to be happy. Remember? Well, if you want her to react that way again, try doing what you did back then. Play!

You can also try to re-create the early dates—in time, place, or activity. Maybe you can't go back to that little town where you met, but if your first date was a movie at the local theater, try a movie today (rent that first one you saw together if you can get it). If it was a dance, find a dance place that features the style of music popular when you dated. It if was a restaurant, try to replicate it.

If you can, do take her back to that original spot. It could be a great anniversary present.

Recalling those scenes in which she was fun and responsive will help you determine some of the subtle ways you can bring her to those feelings again.

The idea is to keep the spirit of those days. Recapture the excitement.

Date at Home

Even a date at home now and then can add sparkle to a relationship. Invite her to dinner—in her own dining room. Bring in flowers, candles, and fix up a feast—or bring home luscious carryouts. Pull out her chair for her when you're ready for her to sit down. Put her napkin on her lap. Keep her glass filled with whatever she's drinking. Let soft music play in the background (no ads please!). And as soon as she's finished, clear her plates from the table. Clean up the kitchen while she relaxes. After dinner turn up the music and take her dancing in the living room. Kick off your shoes and have a good time.

One of our survey respondents told us how she and her husband trade "dinners in" with their neighbors:

On the first Friday of every month, Bill and I dress up as if we were going to a nice restaurant. Our next-door neighbors make a great dinner and bring it over for us—a four-course meal—complete with flowers and candles. They set everything up, light the candles, take the kids, and leave us to each other. We return the dishes and pick up the kids late Saturday morning. Then on the third Friday of each month, we take dinner to them and bring their kids over to play with ours. That's fun, too, because Bill and I have taken some cooking classes and we get to show off what we can do. Of course we make our own dinner at the same time we're making theirs. So we have at least two terrific dinners at home each month. And even when we're making dinner for them, we have fun making it together.

Another respondent offered this: "We recently installed a big Jacuzzi on our deck. And now every Friday night we have a 'date' in the Jacuzzi."

Activities to Hone Your Romantic Spirit

- Write down the place where you met and then make a list of everything you can remember about the event. Add similar significant information about other romantic times together. Take a look at the whole picture and determine if any of that can be replicated today. But don't forget to let her know how exciting she is today. Don't leave her with the impression of "Those were the days . . ."
- Go to your local library or bookstore and pick up the latest copy of Emily Post's *Etiquette* and try on some new manners. You can either start slowly, adding a manner a week, for example, or you can shock her with a whole new you and make her laugh—or swoon! (Use your new-found manners on your mother and your daughter, as well.)
- Purchase or tape some romantic music to play during dinner at home.
- If you're too strapped for money to go anywhere special, start a fund to save for special evenings. And in the meantime, investigate inexpensive activities in your community.

- Make a date with your partner for a special evening—something for which you need to dress up. Pay special attention to your grooming and clothes. Have the car cleaned. Pick up a bouquet of flowers to present to her when you greet her at the door (even if you have to make an excuse to go outside first!). Help her on with her coat. Hold her arm down the driveway. Open her door first and wait until she's in and cozy before you close it. Get into the car and lean over and give her a kiss. Tell her you're the luckiest man in the world. Be sure to pay the same attention to her all evening. Then, the following day, call her and tell her what a wonderful time you had with her. And mark your calendar for the next special event.

- Ask her for an afternoon date: a bike ride, a picnic by the lake (you make the picnic), a day at the beach, a window-shopping stroll through town (note what interests her), a walk in the country (find her a flower or pine cone or fallen leaf), a snowy play day in the backyard . . . get creative.

- Call her up and pretend you've never met her (though of course she'll know that it's you). Tell her that a mutual friend gave you her number and that you want to invite her on a blind date. Plan when and where to meet. Describe yourself and what you will wear (a carnation in your lapel?) and ask her to describe herself. And when you meet, carry the charade as far as you dare. Let her know you want to get to know her better, that you enjoy her company, that you'd like to see her again soon . . .

- After dinner one evening, invite her out for a stroll down the sidewalk—even if it's raining or snowing. Just bundle up and have a good time.

- Send an invitation in the mail to her for a special event (refer to Chapter 5, "Love Notes").

- Before a special evening date, invite her to go shopping with you so that you can help her choose a new outfit to wear on the occasion.

- Plan to surprise your partner when she's off by herself. Casually "run into" her one day when she's out shopping or off on her own, or wait for her after work and approach her in her office parking lot or at the train depot. Try to pick her up as if you don't know her. Tell her you've been watching her from across the room (or across the street) and you couldn't resist coming over to meet her. Offer to take her somewhere and buy her a drink. Tell her your lover is away for the night and you'd like her to come over.
- If you're in the habit of watching television after dinner each evening, try turning it off. Romance happens.

Live in the Present

Why is tomorrow so much more important than today? You're here today and you're probably healthier and more capable of enjoying today than you will be tomorrow.

Too many relationships are based upon the future: saving for retirement, the kids, the living room furniture, or waiting for the next raise or position. Some couples spend their entire lives working and saving for later—and when later comes, the relationship has deteriorated, the children are gone, the couple may even be in poor health.

What is the future that you really want? If you take time to build your relationship through the years, you can look forward to being with someone who wants to spend her time with you as you mature together. Enjoy your time together today, and you will reap the reward of a good relationship lasting into the future.

According to Dr. William Betcher in his book *Intimate Play,* "A man who is in touch with the child inside himself is the ultimate turn-on, because he possesses so many traits that women find attractive. He is playful, imaginative, and has the ability to dream. He is honest, curious, compassionate, and has the ability to enjoy the present."

And Dr. Betcher later adds: "Years spent with the same person though, can imprison both of you in numbing routine, so that you are sleepwalking through much of your time together. You can use play to transform small occurrences into intimate events. The trick is to focus your attention on the present moment, in which opportunities for sharing will often present themselves."

In changing any attitude, behaviorist psychologists have found that if you start by changing the *behavior,* the *attitude* will follow. Putting this in the context of romance, if you try a few new romantic moves with your partner, you will soon *become* a more romantic person. You will become new. Start playing, start acting romantic, and you will become a romantic.

Shake it up. Surprise her. And you'll surprise yourself at how change can stimulate new and special feelings.

You have nothing to lose.

Activities to Hone Your Romantic Spirit

- Take a day off this week to do nothing. (Some companies prefer that you take "mental health" days when you're well—so that you won't have to take even more time off being sick.) Spend it with her if you like, or spend it alone so that you'll be fresh and be ready for her when she's ready for you.
- Take her to an amusement park and hug on the roller coaster or kiss on top of the Ferris wheel.
- Bring her breakfast in bed. Include a little menu. Put the morning paper or whatever book she's currently reading on the tray. A fresh flower is nice, too. And if you want to go all out, iron the linen napkin and put it into the silver napkin ring. But even if it's just her favorite cereal in the old chipped bowl, she'll appreciate the romance of it.
- Spend one week pretending you're the most romantic, desirable guy around. You're suave, handsome—and even wealthy, if that's important to you. Every woman is dying to

be with you. But you don't need any of them—you already have the most wonderful woman. When you greet your partner, sweep her off her feet—kiss her, hug her. Give her a sexy low-throttle "mmmm." And a look that says you want her—and that you know she wants you. Feel it! You're Clark Gable . . . Humphrey Bogart . . . Mel Gibson . . . whoever. (After all, some of the sexiest men make themselves attractive by their attitudes—you can do that too.) Exude that confidence. Playact today . . . and you may just find tomorrow that this is the real you.

4

Romance As Aphrodisiac

If every time you and your partner meet, she greets you with "Hi Honey, let's do it . . . !" you can skip this chapter.

Most of our survey respondents, however, told us that passion is not that easy to achieve.

A woman needs to clear her mind of daily worries in order to focus on sex. And she needs to feel good about herself. Maybe you already knew this. But did you know that you have the power to make it happen?

Your partner needs to know that you find her attractive. Whether she considers herself overweight and out of style, or whether she just made the cover of *Glamour* magazine, she needs to know that *you* think she is gorgeous.

So how do you do that?

Pay attention to her.

To please a woman sexually—and keep her coming back—*forethought* must precede *foreplay*. Why? Because women do not view sex as an isolated event. Passion does not begin when you turn out the lights. Your partner is not going to be in the mood for sex simply because you show up. Her love and passion need nurturing throughout the relationship.

As one of our survey respondents wrote, "A woman who feels wanted is going to please the man who makes her feel wanted."

Women have told us that they appreciate an empathetic ear to rid themselves of all their daily cares. They need a feeling of closeness, caring, and understanding in order to be fully open to enjoying sex with their partners. In order to keep your partner sexually interested, you need to pay attention to her emotional needs as well as her physical needs.

For women, romance is not cause and effect. It's not like a faucet that can be easily turned on at will. For women, romantic experiences have a cumulative effect: the more romantic your experiences with her over time, the more willing she will be for "romance" when you want it.

As one woman wrote:

> My biology teacher once said that men who want to be successful in romance must understand an important principle that differentiates the sexes: Men, like gas stoves, can quickly and easily produce a flame and then quickly cool; whereas women, like electric stoves, are slow to warm up and just as slow to cool down.

And from another: "If couples find little time for romance, they probably have little time for sex, either. It's a way of life. Women like to take their time."

In fact, our survey brought a number of complaints about the way men approach lovemaking. And this may come as a surprise for men: the difference between a lover who pleases his partner and one who doesn't has nothing to do with the man's physical attributes. Instead, it resides in the way a man treats his partner. A good lover is one who not only enjoys sex himself, but who also desires to give his partner love and pleasure. You've got to be good to her.

This chapter is not a sex manual, for enough of those already exist. Rather, it offers ways to inspire a more sensual connection. And for a woman, that's where a good sexual relationship begins.

Be Her Romantic Hero

The romantic heroes are not the ones who fill the screen with immediate sexual gratification. Instead, the romantic knows how to play the scene, set the mood, take the time to enliven sensual desires in the woman he loves. Romance carries sexual overtones, to be sure, and it often culminates in a sexual encounter. But most of all, romance is a prolonged feeling filled with flirtation, sensuality, and longing. How do you establish such a feeling?

Flirt with Her

Whether you have just met that special woman or you've been sleeping beside her for years, you can't underestimate the power of flirting. The eyes, the smiles, the winks, the little words that tell your partner you want her. This sets the mood.

Flirting is often the first stage of foreplay, the beginning of a glorious tension, which builds until you *must* have each other. In order to reach that point, flirting takes restraint. You each hold back from taking your pleasure until you *both* want it.

As one of our respondents wrote:

> I love it when he's playful, looking at me sideways, smiling in that winking sort of way, noticing every little thing about me. It makes me playful, too.

Although the majority of our respondents find playfulness important to romance, less than half of them get enough.

Flirting received particularly high marks from younger women as well as from women with children. Since mothers put so much energy into attending to children—rather than to themselves—these women especially appreciate flirtatious attention. It helps affirm their attractiveness.

If you feel uncomfortable about flirting with your partner, go back to Chapter 3, "Romance Every Day," and reread the section entitled "Court Her."

But don't save flirting until you're ready for sex. You should be flirting with your partner every day. Protracted foreplay, you might call it—hours or even days in advance of sex. Even if she hasn't been "in the mood" lately, she's sure to come around with enough flirting.

As one of our survey respondents wrote:

> He takes me seriously when I have a serious concern. And I appreciate that. But when the concern is relieved—usually through his listening—he is so much fun. He watches my eyes. He hears me. He makes me smile. He responds to my signals, touches me in ways that tell me that he cares—not that he cares because he wants sex, but that he cares about pleasing me. That's romantic.

Pay attention to the way *she* flirts back. And read between the lines, for she's sure to be letting you know when she's ready, and what she wants.

Touch Her

In order to find out what women want from their sexual partner, we asked them what makes them feel sexy, what makes them want more. The response that came again and again, more than any other, was touching—loving but *nonsexual* touching—anytime, anywhere. Hugging, cuddling, kissing. When touching is practiced as a way of life, it shows that you enjoy being close with your partner.

Nonsexual touching creates an intimacy from which sex naturally flows. Our findings, which told us that sex is too often a physical routine, lacking romance, lacking the wonderful pleasure that it could be, also told us that nonsexual touching can bring more romance to a sexual relationship than any new sexual position or repertoire.

This is the sort of touching that women find romantic: "brushing a strand of hair from my face," "brushing my hair," "having his hands tangled in my hair," "kissing me behind the ear," "touching my face," "when he sits close to me and puts his arm around my shoulder," "his hand on my thigh when we sit next to each other at the movies, at dinner, on the couch

watching a video," "some sort of sweet physical contact whenever we're together."

Subtle stuff. Women love it.

If a woman is emotionally ready, then having her bare skin
touched anywhere on her body can be exciting. Here's what
one of our respondents wrote:

> We were on our evening walk. We stopped at the top of the hill and
> when I turned toward him, he ran his hand along my cheek. Then
> he stroked my hair. Suddenly, I wanted him.

What too many women are missing is "lots of touching and
kissing—all over my body."

A very special form of touching is massage. Massage does
not necessarily lead to sex. But through massage, you can help
your partner get in touch with the sensuality of her own body.
Giving your partner a good long massage also lets your partner
know that you enjoy touching her body and spending intimate
time with her.

Though some women prefer a little rougher handling
once aroused, our survey respondents rated "He touches me
with tenderness" as the single thing they found most romantic.

Look at Her

Have you ever been driving down the freeway and, when you
happen to look at the car next to you, the other driver looks
back at you? There's something riveting about someone watching you. It doesn't go unnoticed.

As one of our survey respondents said, "I love it when he
looks at me that special way that lets me know he wants me,
even after all these years."

This is most effective if you also practice sweet talking,
touching, and flirting on a regular basis. Smile at her as she
walks across the room. Keep your eyes on her as she sits,

stands, moves. Notice everything about her. Look at all aspects of her body: the curves, the turns, the way it moves.

Watching without flirting will unnerve her. She may think that you've noticed the run in her stocking or her chipped nail. To put her at ease, let your eyes smile at her. Say something complimentary so that she knows you're thinking how beautiful she is. Just one little compliment will help her relax.

When she speaks, hold eye contact for a while—as long as it feels comfortable. And then after looking away for a moment, come back to it. This will not only show her that you're paying attention to her, but it will also help you focus on what she is saying. And do listen—for she may be telling you what she wants.

"When he watches me, that's when I know he's appreciating my body," wrote one of our survey respondents. "That makes me feel sexy. That makes me want him to want me."

This sort of attention will also help your partner focus on you—and make it easier for her to respond. For some women, all this attention may even be an invitation to show off a bit, which will only add to the fun. As one of our respondents wrote:

> I caught him watching me undress, sort of smiling in that coy way
> of his that let me know he was interested, so I turned around and
> gave him a real slow strip. I think he liked it. Oh yeah!

Activities to Hone Your Romantic Spirit

Following are examples of actions and activities which, according to our survey respondents, express the romantic spirit. Try one or two now, and them come back later for more when you feel comfortable enough to take a few more risks.

- Practice paying attention to her any time that you're together—while she dresses in the morning, when you're together during the day or evening, while you eat together, when she undresses at night. Let her know you're paying attention. Tell her what it is about her in particular that pleases you.

- Make a date to meet your partner in the middle of the day—for lunch, shopping, whatever—and put all your energy into flirting with her.
- Write her an erotic note or letter and mail it to her.
- When in a restaurant, share your food. Feed her, and let her feed you. Think sensual.
- Touch her in a nonsexual way at least once every day. Vary the ways and places you touch her.
- The next time you have time enough for a good long sexual session, try prolonging foreplay until *she* must have *you.*
- Try nibbling, licking, or gently biting some part of her body that you have ignored in the past. Watch her reaction to know whether you should pay more attention to it in the future. And next time, try another area.
- If you don't already know how to give her a good massage, take a class or buy a book on the subject and teach yourself. Then surprise her with a terrific long, slow one.

Create an Atmosphere for Love

Creating a sensual atmosphere conducive to intimacy is a terrific way to show your partner that you care enough about *her,* not just about sex.

According to our respondents, the proper ambiance does indeed enhance lovemaking.

In his book *The New Male–Female Relationship,* Dr. Herb Goldberg, clinical psychologist, says that while men are conditioned to be sexual, women are conditioned to be sensual. So if you want this to be a special time, set a scene that will encourage her sensuality. Creating the right atmosphere is not just a matter of going to a special place or treating her to a grand event. It involves attention to what makes her *feel sexy.*

Even Koco the gorilla refuses to mate unless the setting is quiet and private. (Her owners have shipped her to Maui for the proper romantic setting.)

Stimulate Her Senses

With a little planning, you can create attitudes and moods that will let your partner know she is not only desired but also desirable. Stimulate her senses. If she's like most of our survey respondents, she will appreciate low lighting, a warm temperature, soft fabrics, soft music, a cool drink, and a slow hand.

The focus should be on her. Get rid of all distractions ahead of time. Turn off the TV. Take care of the children and pets. Let her feel that she can relax and enjoy her time with you.

When querying women about atmospheres conducive to sex, we found that lighting is particularly important. Maybe it's a soft living room light, a fire in the fireplace, or a candle next to the bed. Sunset and sunrise are romantic, as are moonlight and starlight. Soft, low light—particularly reddish tones—will give you both a soft glow of elegance.

One woman wrote:

> Some men seem to like the lights full up so you can see everything. Maybe they think that's flattering. But for me, it's only inhibiting. Full light reveals every flaw. Maybe I'm too self-conscious about my flaws, but I think that I'm not unusual among women who were brought up to believe that makeup, special underwear, and high heels help them to look glamorous, and that nothing short of glamorous is attractive. I'm sorry, but if I don't feel attractive, I don't feel sexy. And under a bright lighting situation, I just can't enjoy myself. I'm too worried about what he's thinking he would rather see than me.

This woman reveals not only that lighting is important, but also that making a woman feel attractive, in whatever lighting, helps her feel comfortable about herself—comfortable enough to be sexy.

Wear something soft to the touch: a flannel or silk shirt or a terry bathrobe. Of course you're clean and well groomed, clean-shaven, with nice breath. And if she likes cologne, wear a bit (but don't overpower her with too much scent).

Make a cozy place to cuddle. Offer her something to eat or drink—something light, not too filling. Play her favorite music, soft enough so that it does not interfere with conversation.

Give Her Time

Start leisurely. Let her relax and absorb the situation. Take time to do it right. Be playful. And give her a chance to get into the mood, to start to play along.

Compliment her: the way she looks, the way she smells.

Listen to her. Encourage her. Acknowledge her. Kiss her ear. Speak to her in a low soft voice. Let your warm breath caress her inner ear.

Invite her for a slow close dance around the living room. Kiss her neck, caress her with your hands, whisper to her while you're dancing. Use sensual sexy words. Hold her body against yours. Try a few erotic dance moves.

Massage her neck—gently, softly. Take off one of her shoes and massage her foot. Maybe loosen a piece of her clothing, and softly . . . slowly . . . touch her skin as you do so. Tell her how wonderful she looks, smells, sounds, feels, tastes; how soft her skin feels, how lovely the shape of her ankle, her calf, or whatever it is you are touching; and how wonderful you feel when you are with her.

Help her feel sexy, desirable, lovable. Tell her intimate things you love about her.

Make her feel safe. She doesn't need drugs or alcohol to feel uninhibited. She needs trust.

One of our survey respondents shared the wonderful way in which her partner creates an atmosphere for sex and intimacy. Take note. This is a lover who knows how to please.

> He greets me at the door with a kiss and a hug and "Oh Gloria, how wonderful to see you."

I talk about my work and he listens. Maybe I had a bad day or maybe I've got an exciting new project. I want to talk. He knows I like to talk. He knows me well. He listens.

He asks me about my project and I tell him this and that and as I speak he looks into my eyes. He takes off my shoes and massages my calves and yet he listens and listens and listens and responds to what I say and he knows I get a stiff neck when I'm tense so he starts massaging my neck and stroking my hair, my cheek.

And so it goes until he's totally cleared my mind of my bad day or my new project or the office politics or the gossip and rumors and who knows what and he's still ready to listen.

Once my mind is cleared of my concerns, he's looking pretty good to me. I lean back on the couch and he brings me a glass of wine. I unbutton his shirt.

He kisses my neck and my cheek.

I put his hand on my breast.

And then it's all kissing and touching all over, making me want him and want him and want him. And he's undressing me with "Oh Gloria, my favorite little panties . . ." and by now my body is only responding to my desires. Which he fulfills—oh yes!—quite nicely.

Maybe it will be sex tonight or maybe it will have to wait. Take your time. Take your cues from her. Romance is cumulative—it builds, like a good investment. Keep investing.

Think sensual. Touch, smell, taste, look, feel. Pay attention to *her* signals. And you're sure to please her.

Sweet Talk Her

Unless your partner is unusual, she probably will not become sexually aroused from conversations about sports, your job, her job, the children, the pets, the neighbors, your bad back, the things that need repair, the dirty dishes in the sink, the dust under the bed, relatives. . . .

Instead, use "sweet talk."

Sweet-talk subjects include anything sensual: music, art, literature (especially erotic or sensual literature), food and wine, nature, colors, fabrics, sex. Most importantly, sweet talk is about your partner.

Use a soft, low voice. Use passionate words that tell her that you want her. Keep the focus on her. Tell her wonderful things about her body—the way it looks, the way it smells, the way it reacts to your touch. Tell her how you want to make love to her.

Whisper words that make her feel that you are enjoying every moment with her.

Stay in the present. Don't talk about past or future. Don't think about past or future.

Share Fantasies

Fantasize. If you're both willing, you might tell her some of your sexual fantasies—starring *her*, of course. And if she's game, encourage her to open up about her fantasies as well. These might be stories or merely sexual images.

Let her play a role for you: the bank president in the Board room, the little girl on the swing, whatever you know will turn *her* on.

And if she reveals her fantasies to you, don't judge them as silly, weird, or dumb. Instead, follow through. If you haven't done this before, take it slowly, since things may come up that could embarrass or offend either of you.

You might even want to collaborate, get into a fantasy together. Start an erotic story in which each of you has a role. "Through the window I watched as she slowly unbuttoned her dress," you might begin. Let her take the part of the woman being watched.

If you think that she will enjoy it, talk dirty. But don't insist or embarrass her if it's not to her liking. (Our survey respondents got *more* of this than they desired.) Above all else, show respect for her. Intimacy comes only when partners respect themselves, their relationship, and each other.

Activities to Hone Your Romantic Spirit

- Find out in which atmospheres your partner can feel most free to be sexy. Try different rooms. Test different lighting, music, foods, scented candles, times of day. Try wearing different types of clothing—jeans and a flannel shirt, good slacks and a silk shirt, a smoking jacket, silk boxer shorts— and see how she reacts.
- Invite her for a dance around the living room. Slow dancing is conducive to touching, kissing, caressing. Take advantage of it.
- Buy a book of love poetry and choose a few appropriate ones to read to her.
- Call her up and make sensuous love on the phone. Use a low sexy voice. Tell her what it is about her that excites you. Tell her you're thinking about her sexy body and describe sexy things you're looking forward to doing with her. Let your imagination go wild and tell her what you're imagining she is doing while you speak. If she has a *very private* phone at home or at her office, leave the message on her answering machine.
- Make an erotic tape for her—your voice telling her wonderful things about her body and how good she makes you feel.
- Buy a book of erotic stories and choose one to read to her tonight. Let her choose one to read to you tomorrow.
- At a party or some public setting, whisper erotic somethings into her ear, kiss her neck, put your arm around her when you introduce her to your friends or when she introduces you to hers.

Practice Foreplay

If you think of foreplay as a rush to the finish line, you will rob yourself—as well as your partner—of an essential part of sexual pleasure. This is the fine tension, the play of light and dark, the emotional capability that differentiates humans from other animals. For a woman, foreplay is a show of affection. And it can be a reassurance that you truly enjoy being with her. So do—enjoy it.

But what is foreplay, anyway? It is prolonged stimulation that promotes physical arousal. Prolonged. That's key. But that does not necessarily mean hours of foreplay just before you want sex. Prolonged means cumulative, over days even weeks, of romantic looks, touches, sweet talk, interludes. If a woman's romantic desires are satisfied on a daily basis, she may not need extended foreplay immediately prior to sex. On the other hand, if a woman is ignored until she is sexually "wanted," she will need enough foreplay to know that she is cared for, desired, desirable, beautiful, intelligent, etc. etc. etc. So best not to wait until the elevator has reached the eleventh floor.

When you are interested in sexually arousing your partner, you may want to begin with flirting, along with nonsexual touching and kissing (her hair, her neck, her shoulder). Prolong the contact there before gradually moving to more sexually sensitive erogenous zones—those areas lush with sensory nerves.

Undressing your partner as a form of touching can be quite exciting to her—either slowly removing one garment now and another later as part of foreplay, or undressing her all at once in a passionate rush when she's fully aroused. And because nudity can become boring, leaving on a bit of her lingerie can add to the excitement for both of you.

When we asked survey respondents to rate the statement, "He undresses me with loving care, awe, wonder," seventy-four percent of our respondents rated it as *very important,* but only twenty-three percent said they were getting enough of it.

Every woman is different, however, and the most sexually stimulating area of one woman's body may not be the most stimulating for the next. It is important for you to discover what your own partner desires—which touches relax her and which arouse her. If she hasn't verbalized this, just watching her response to your own moves will help you learn what pleases her.

Show Her the Real Thing

Numerous books have been written for men to help them physically please a woman. One woman might say do it this way, while another says she wants something else. Our survey underlined the fact that unless you're out to please the masses, statistics don't count. Statistics can only generalize. It's what your own love wants that matters. Finding out what *she* wants is key.

How well do you know what your partner wants? Chances are, she may desire sexual stimulations of which you are unaware. Maybe even she isn't aware of them herself. After all, if she hasn't experienced them yet, how would she know?

To find out how to please her sexually, take a look at the questions in Chapter 10, "Your Romance Notebook." If you don't know the answers, find out—either by asking her or by "trial and pleasure."

If you're unsure about what to try or how to please her in ways different from what she is accustomed to, you may want to invest in a good book about the subject. *The Magic of Sex,* by Miriam Stoppard, M.D., is a good place to start.

But remember, no matter what any book tells you, every woman is unique. There may have been women in your past who enjoyed this or that, or you may have read or seen films about women's secret sex spots or positions that would drive any woman wild. (Don't even mention these things to your partner because they are not at all relevant to your relationship with her and, worst of all, she may interpret this as a comparison with what she should be.) Respect the special desires of you own partner and learn what *she* wants.

Most important, when making love, let your partner know that you appreciate *her.* Our survey respondents told us what they like about the way their partners make love to them. A few examples:

> When he talks to me during lovemaking, letting me know that he wants me and why and how I turn him on. Tell me more!

> Eye contact. When we're kissing. When we're loving. I love to see the expression in his eyes, because when he's loving me his expression is always so caring.

> When making love, he touches my face, says my name, plays with my hair. It makes me feel that he's glad he's with ME.

> What turns me on? Kissing that doesn't get to anything more until I can't stand it!

Break Through the Envelope

If you're in the right place and she's in the right place and everything is working for you, sex can be exhilarating. But as one of our survey respondents noted: "Let's face it, sometimes sex is just plain boring."

Ok, so maybe you've gotten into a rut. You both know when it's going to happen and so you take your positions, take on your roles, and boom boom boom. And then you go to sleep. Romantic? Not!

Fortunately, many of our survey respondents shared ways in which they were able to break out of old sex habits and create a new excitement.

Create Lovemaking Styles

If lovemaking is all quickies, your partner will become angry and frustrated. But if you have to spend hours in foreplay every time, sex may begin to feel like work.

One solution to sexual boredom and frustration is to create a number of different lovemaking styles. Vary the amount of time you spend in each lovemaking session. You don't always need to create a sensual and passionate romantic atmosphere.

Dr. William Betcher touches on this in his book *Intimate Play:*

> There is a truth concealed here about play and sexuality: humans, unlike three-spined sticklebacks and fruit flies, have the potential for two distinct kinds of sexual intimacy—one that requires you to take your time, to dance around your lover, and to be open to the sort of loose mental connection that makes humor possible; and one that takes the shortest line between two organs and presses for ripsnorting, instinctual release. I would not want to do without either of them. A good friend of mine told me that the joy he felt in getting his partner to laugh at his wordplay was associated with a feeling of potency very similar to the satisfaction of facilitating her orgasm. My wish for you, then, is many orgasms but just as much laughter, even if they never happen at the same time.

If you spend fifteen minutes in foreplay with your partner this time, she may be game for a quickie the next time.

As one of our survey respondents wrote:

> After years of marriage, we've learned to keep sex exciting by using different kinds of ways to make love. We have our typical twenty-minute sessions; our "quickies"; and our special times when we create a sensual atmosphere and engage in prolonged foreplay. We have also developed "sex" vacations—taking off together for a romantic night or weekend where we can focus on intimacy and refresh our sex life.

One lovemaking style that many women say they would like more is spontaneous sex. In spite of all the talk about preparing the right atmosphere, getting her in the mood, and playing your hand slowly, surprise: an unfulfilled desire common among our survey respondents was "sex right now because we're both hot."

This does not mean more "quickies." Spontaneous sex is very nonroutine sex that happens in out-of-the-ordinary circumstances, when you let her know that you just have to have her. And forty percent of our survey respondents told us that they weren't getting enough of it.

The key is play. Flirt to test the waters. If it happens, it happens; if not, then try it again, another time. A few examples from some of our survey respondents:

> We were making dinner together. The kids were asleep. The music was playing. I was tossing the salad. "I feel like tossing your sweet ass," he told me as he came up behind me and kissed me on the neck and held my breasts and I dropped the salad tongs and sighed and, well, it all happened right there in the kitchen, and afterward we got back to what we were doing. I smile whenever I think of it.

> We were so relieved to drive away from the party where our friends Don and Mary were tedious to the point of why are we here? They were arguing, encouraging us to take sides. Our response (finally alone together), on the way home, was to celebrate all the things good about our own relationship. He drove, I talked. I moved closer and began kissing his neck. He began fondling me. I responded in kind. He pulled over in the dark under the trees and—with all the doors locked—we escaped to the back of the van and got it rocking. Pretty hot stuff for a gray-haired couple.

Just don't get arrested.

And keep in mind, no matter how fast a sexual event, our survey confirms that women appreciate an approach that includes kissing, hugging, and touching *before* the flag is raised. Take advantage of all you know about flirting, sweet talking, and foreplay—just move it along a lot faster. Touching her face, kissing her neck, whispering in her ear don't take much time, but they can add a great deal to her pleasure. Even when sex will take only five minutes, letting her know that you want her—not just sex—will make it more pleasurable for both of you.

Replay the Best of Times

If your sex life has lost some of the magic you once knew, then think back on what made it special, and try to re-create some of those earlier scenes. What did you wear, what did she wear? What did you say? How did you touch her? How did you excite her?

When queried about sexual fantasies, a common response involved meeting a stranger. But before you get too worried, here's an example:

> It would probably involve some man I've never met, which seems totally unfair to my husband, who really is a great guy. I was carried away with the whole meeting-and-falling-desperately-in-love experience. And I wouldn't mind going back and doing that all over again. Maybe amnesia could be arranged?

It's not that your partner wants someone new, it's that she wants a more romantic relationship with *you*.

You've heard the old adage "Actions speak louder than words." Show by your actions that she is *the* most important part of your life. Treat her as well as you would an important client, a significant event, a critical meeting. Your relationship with her is much deeper and longer lasting than any of those. Let her feel that.

Let her know that she's worth the trouble.

Treat her the way you did when you were courting. Look as attractive as you can—shave and cologne yourself *before* you approach her rather than when you leave her. Pay attention to what you wear (soft), and how you smell (sexy).

Invest in a pair of sexy pajamas—for yourself. A pair of silk boxer shorts, a silk robe, or a smoking jacket might be appropriate. Most department stores carry these and other such items in the men's department.

Try Something New

Try having sex in a different place in the house, in the backyard, or in a different locale entirely. Make love at a different time of day: at noon, before dinner, in the middle of the night.

Among the romantic fantasies that our survey respondents shared, certain aspects were common: making love in water, such as in a bathtub or spa, at a lake, or in the ocean waves; making love in special lighting circumstances, such as in front of a fire, in the moonlight, at daybreak, or with candles; and making love in unusual settings, such as in a limousine, on the beach, or in the back room at a party. If you think that your partner would enjoy something a little bit different, why not give it a try? Be creative.

Tell her why she is a wonderful lover. Be specific. What does she—and only she—do that makes you go crazy? Help her to feel that she is the only woman in the world who can make you feel this way.

Try a fantasy. Tell her that tonight she's your mistress. Or tell her you're trying to get her in bed for the first time. Work at it. Or pretend you've just met and you just can't control yourself. Know what will excite her and try it.

Encourage her to invest in some sexy lingerie. If she is not in the habit of wearing sexy things, it may be because she feels her body is not sexy enough. Or it may be because she feels such things are frivolous. When she puts it on, respond positively. Do the most serious flirting you've ever done. Imagine that she's the woman you've watched from across the room all night and here she comes, over to you, and you've got about a minute to let her know that *you want her.* Watch her respond.

Rent an erotic video (not pornographic, in other words, sensual rather than hardcore) and watch it together. Invest in a book of erotic (not pornographic) stories and read them aloud to each other.

Experiment touching your partner in different places or in different ways than you have in the past.

Try using positions you haven't used for a while—or try new ones.

Spend an evening just kissing, hugging, and petting, the way you did when you were a teenager.

Purchase new sheets: white lacy things or dark erotic satins.

Invest in some scented oils to add to the sensuality of your massages.

Have Sex with Food

Feed each other while making love. Have sex with food . . . or food with sex. Have fun.

Even though our survey respondents did not list candy as a desirable gift, a number of women told us that they find sharing chocolate with their partner to be especially erotic: chocolate in a hot tub, chocolate with champagne, chocolate in bed. If you think your partner may tend toward that particular pleasure, keep a box of special chocolates within easy reach.

Be Private in Public

When you're out with others, make sure you let her know that she's the one you want to be with.

Here's what our survey respondents had to say:

I love it when we're in public and he whispers something to me that makes me blush.

Conspiratorial looks or glances across a crowded room . . . make me want to kiss him.

Sexy moves when others aren't looking—the way he sips at his beer, for example, even at a Fourth of July picnic, licking his lips in that slow sexy way, moving his torso just so. If anyone saw him, they'd cart him away. But I'd rescue him real quick.

Invest in Afterplay

And don't forget *afterplay*.

Snuggling after making love was on the top of our respondent's romance list, right up there with touching. This is a *very important* widely held desire.

After lovemaking, hold on to the intimacy. Stay in the present with her. Not only will this please her now, but it will help pave the way to your next encounter.

We heard from too many of our survey respondents that men too often turn away after sex and fall asleep. "It's like eat and run," wrote one woman.

Instead, say a few soft words that let her know how much pleasure she gives you. Hang on to her. Cuddle.

Remember: romance is cumulative. If you want to have your way next time, do it right this time.

Activities to Hone Your Romantic Spirit

- Make a list of ten sexual encounters you would enjoy. They may be new places to have sex, new positions, new times— whatever you might desire. Ask your partner to make a similar list. Then share your ideas.
- Try initiating sex in a different way from what you have done in the past.
- Look at the questions in Chapter 10, "Your Romance Notebook." Learn all the answers to what pleases your partner.
- Based upon what you both desire, create a repertoire of lovemaking styles.
- While making love, focus on her. Touch her all over. Fondle her. Take your time. Concentrate your attention on her. Show passion. Stay in the present.

- Undress her slowly . . . taking time to appreciate every part of her body. And as you peel the clothes from her body, kiss the newly exposed skin, touch it, fondle it. Love it. Breathe in the scent of her hair, her skin. Touch the soft curves of her body. Whisper how excited she makes you. No need to take everything off. Leaving a few small garments for later can add to the fun.
- If she undresses you, keep your focus on her. Watch what she does, respond likewise.
- While making love, talk to her in low soft tones. Don't talk about the mechanics of what you're doing. Instead, tell her how wonderful she looks and feels, how great she makes you feel.
- Afterward, hold her, tell her that you love her, cuddle her until she falls asleep.
- If your relationship has been stuck for a long time, or if you want to add some pizzazz to it but are shy to try something new, pretend you're somebody else, someone you consider sexy—a movie star, a Greek god, a romantic hero—someone that makes you feel very sexy. You might want to keep it to yourself, or you might want to add a prop and let her know who you are tonight.

Take Care of Yourself

Being healthy and feeling good about yourself can only help your performance in anything you undertake. So take care of yourself, and encourage your partner to do the same.

This is not to say that you are not attractive unless you look like an athlete, but keeping yourself the best *you* can be will make you most attractive to her.

If you're overweight or know that you consume an unhealthy diet, make some changes. And if you don't exercise regularly, start now. Get your doctor involved, if necessary.

If you have a favorite sport, find out where you can participate in it. Sign up with your local community center for an aerobic exercise class. Join a gym or tennis club, or get yourself a bicycle.

The best lover is a healthy lover—mentally, emotionally, and physically.

Encourage Her to Be Sexy

If a woman thinks she's sexy, she'll be sexy.

A worry all too common among women is physical appearance. Women are bombarded with TV ads and magazine covers of perfect female faces and bodies. It doesn't matter that those faces might have undergone months of surgery or that the bodies may be half silicone and half liposuctioned away.

> Sex? Yikes! Look at me! Bad hair day, my makeup is totally wrong for this light, and flab . . . oh! I need a good three months alone with Richard Simmons before I'll let my partner see me naked again . . .

Most women want to hide parts of their bodies they think are not model-perfect. If a man wants his partner to feel free and happy in sex, he must show her that she need not hide from him. He can teach her that she is beautiful. He can also teach her how to become more sexual.

It's usually a man, in fact, who makes a woman feel beautiful. Help her get rid of all those inhibitions that keep her from enjoying herself fully. As one of our respondents told us:

> I hated my body. Whenever I looked into a mirror, I saw only my small breasts and my large thighs. I was embarrassed to take off my clothes in front of anyone. Sex was always tense for me because I was afraid to be seen from certain angles. But Craig changed all that. He smiled as I undressed. He told me how lovely my body was. He touched me in ways that made me believe that he really meant it. Then I was ok and I could finally relax enough to enjoy sex. Since that time I've learned to even show off a little. And now I'm not afraid to initiate sex myself.

Make her feel beautiful, not just by complimenting everything about her that you find beautiful, but by *showing* her that she's irresistible. As another survey respondent told us:

> Good sex for me means making me feel sexy. How does a man do that? When I'm undressing for bed and he grabs my underwear as I take it off and holds it to his face and inhales it. Well, it doesn't matter that my thighs are going cellulite or my hair's getting gray or I may have even lost my job in the last few months—he WANTS MY BODY. And I feel that fast heat start up my spine and I don't even bother with my nightly ritual of face cream and dental guard. He wants me and I respond—on a number of levels. Nothing could be more sexually stimulating than knowing that a man really wants your body.

Encourage her to look her best. Encourage her to wear sexy clothes. Listen to what women have to say:

> Sexy lingerie. I love to wear it under anything and I feel so sexy. Even at a PTA meeting. And by the time we get home together, I'm already undressing him.

> I love it when he pulls out some of my sexy lingerie and asks me for a show. And I do oblige him . . . !

> Wearing a classy evening dress when we go somewhere special. Everyone notices. I feel special. And I feel that he's happy I'm with him.

If she's out of shape, encourage her to exercise regularly. Help her get on a healthy diet. You can do this without nagging or complaining about the way she looks. Invite her to take a walk with you three evenings a week, for example, or join a gym together, or start a new sport like roller skating or bicycling. Tell her that *you* want to eat healthy—you might start by buying the groceries and cooking a nice healthy dinner for her. Then let her know how great she looks as her body becomes more shapely.

Activities to Hone Your Romantic Spirit

- If you're not in your best shape, start a diet and/or exercise program to get back to feeling good about your body and your health. (If you suffer from ill health or specific physical ailments, be sure to consult with your physician.)
- If your libido suffers from inactivity, try practicing nonsexual touching. Think about investing in books, magazines, films, or other sex stimulants to help you regain your former prowess. Encourage your partner to be sexy.
- If your partner doesn't own sexy lingerie, encourage her to invest in some. To do that, show her a photo in a magazine or a catalog and say, "I'd love to see something like this on you!"

5

Love Notes

The love letter may well be as old as language itself: the sensual drawing in the cave, the watery note in the sand, the greeting scribed on parchment, the initials carved into the tree, the kiss pressed upon the envelope.

The love letter allows the writer to express true feelings without interruption. It provides a medium for a lover to let his true love know that no matter where he is or what he's doing, he's thinking of her. It provides a memento to be read again and again, and then pasted into a scrapbook or locked into a little ribboned box. Most of all, it gives the recipient such pleasure. Our survey respondents rated love notes and love letters at the top of the list of romantic gifts.

Unfortunately, however, with the advent of the telephone, the art of letter writing has all but died. When we think of letters these days, we think of business correspondence and greeting cards.

But what is a love letter anyway, and how does one go about writing one? Now don't panic; you don't need a degree in literature to write a special love message. In fact, you'll need to break a few grammatical rules along the way in order to provide a sense of intimacy.

For starters, try a little love note.

Writing the Little Love Note

Little love notes are always appropriate. Send them often, for no reason at all. Send them to her at home (even if you live together); send them to her office (with "confidential" written plainly across the outside of the envelope); leave them somewhere she'll be sure to find them (in her kitchen cupboard, in her lingerie drawer, on the dashboard of her car . . .). Nearly half of our survey respondents rated love notes as *very romantic,* yet only nine percent said they received enough of them.

What we offer here is an easy formula. It's a jumping-off point to a more individualized communication. And if you don't know where to begin, this easy-to-do formula is where you want to start. No, it's not cheating—it's learning. Because pretty soon you'll be playing with it, embellishing it. And as you obtain more experience, you'll find yourself creating your own style, getting more and more playful, making her smile and laugh and cry over your words.

For short love notes, begin writing just above center on the page. You don't want the note to be all crowded up at the top. Don't bother with formalities such as your return address or her full name and address. Start with the date. Put it near the right-hand corner of the page. Give it a little space.

Then come about one third down the page and write a loving salutation: use the most endearing name you have ever called her—if you have a pet name for her, use it, or come up with a new one. Be creative. "Dearest Adele," "My Sweet Silly Sally," or simply "Darling" is certainly appropriate.

Ok, so now we're ready for the body: Use phrases instead of sentences. Start by telling her that you're thinking of her. A few examples: "Missing you." "Just want to let you know I'm thinking of you." "Remembering last night . . ." That's the first paragraph.

Now start a new paragraph. Tell your partner how much you look forward to being with her. Try something like: "Can't wait to touch you again." "Looking forward to Saturday night." If you're feeling a bit bolder, come up with something more sensuous, such as: "Impatient for the scent of your skin." "Anxious to crush my lips against yours."

Then add a closing: "Till then" "All my love" "Hugs and kisses." Even better would be a private phrase or reference that only the two of you share.

Sign with your favorite pet name or nickname—best if it's something private between the two of you.

Be creative with punctuation—separate your "paragraphs" with commas, periods, exclamation points, dashes, ellipses— or nothing at all.

And that's all there is to it. Pretty simple, eh?

Of course your high-school English teacher would have a fit, but unless she's your partner, who cares? Your lover will love it.

One of our survey respondents told us:

> I had been going out with Michael for a few weeks when I found a small envelope in my purse one day while I was fishing for my car keys. It was a simple note from Michael, telling me that he was anxious to see me again. It made me smile. And I was anxious to see him again, as well.

A husband might leave the following note where his wife will see it when he's not home—either where she'll find it after he leaves the house in the morning or where she'll find it as soon as she comes home from work late in the day (try the refrigerator):

Darling—
Last night and you're still on my mind . . .
So wonderful you are with me.
Ever and ever,
   Craig

A lover might send this to a partner who lives on her own. Or a husband could send it to his wife when one or the other is traveling away from home:

Maria Mia,
The scent of your skin lingering still on my pillow . . .
Refuse to wash it until you return
Hugs & kisses . . .
  Your ever-loving Teddy Bear

Here's another that could be used by a husband who is just leaving on a trip, or a man who lives apart from his lover:

My dearest Belinda,
Just left and missing you already
And ready already for Saturday night.
Till then . . .much love,
  Daryl

And what about the little love note you want to send to someone new, someone you've just met . . . or maybe want to meet? Now that's risky . . . and romantic. It will get her attention, for sure. Have the waiter give this one to the lovely lady seated across the restaurant—write it on a napkin—send it over with a glass of wine (if that's what she's drinking) or a truffle. Even if she's already engaged in another relationship, it will at least make her smile:

My Dear Lovely Lady—
So delicate your manners,
So lovely your eyes . . .
Will you smile for me?
Waiting across the room,
  The man who watches you!

Or maybe you know each other but you're not sure how to approach her—or how she might respond. Be mysterious. And if you give her enough clues, she just may guess that it's you.

Sweet Carmine,
Neighbor of mine
How long I have longed for . . .
Well, how about you?
  A secret admirer

If you're getting the "silent treatment" after an argument, try putting the communication back into your relationship with a fun little note:

Chrissy Darling—
Of course you're right
(though maybe I am, too)
But let's not waste another moment apart.
  Your man in waiting

If she's actually left you, a little love note may be just the final romantic touch that will bring her back:

Joanna Baby—
No food no sleep
No thoughts except of you . . .
Hurry back . . .
Ever & always,
  Buster

And don't be afraid to add a little humor:

Oh Sylvia—
Miss your cooking
The house is a mess
If you come back honey
I'll buy you a dress.
  J.J.

Activities to Hone Your Romantic Spirit

Following are examples of actions and activities which, according to our survey respondents, express the romantic spirit. Try one or two now, and then come back later for more when you feel comfortable enough to take a few more risks.

- Write a love note for no reason. Put it where she'll find it when you're away.
- Write a love note thanking her for doing something wonderful for you. Send it in the mail.

- Write her a love note after you've had a particularly wonderful time on a "date." Tell her what fun you had. Leave it where she'll find it.
- Think of new, romantic ways to sign your notes: "Your truest love," "Your ever-loving husband," "Your love slave." (If she hasn't given you a love name, make one up and try it out as your signature on a love note.)

Creating Longer Love Letters

Unlike the little love note, the love letter generally does have a purpose, and it can take a number of forms: it can be persuasive, apologetic, or simply informative. All love letters, however, share common aspects that make them romantic:

- A loving personal greeting (as intimate as possible);
- A mention of the loved one in each paragraph (about missing her, or remembering something wonderful about her, or hoping for something to come);
- A loving closing paragraph (as intimate as possible);
- An intimate signature.

As with the short love note, don't bother with your return address or her full name and address. Start with the date. Put it near the right-hand corner of the page. Leave a little space (not as much as with the love note) and begin as you would with a love note: with an endearing salutation.

For your letter, however, you'll want to use at least some actual sentences. But don't be afraid to be creative. Break it up now and then with a phrase or clause used as a sentence. Use short paragraphs. And number your pages.

If you know a language other than English (even if she doesn't), throw in a few foreign words here and there. She'll have fun trying to decipher your message. Just make sure it will be interpreted properly.

If the two of you are separated by time or distance, begin by telling her that you miss her, that you're thinking of her; use specifics: I miss hearing your voice, I miss your smiling eyes, I miss your kisses. Then go ahead and tell her what you've been doing, how you're feeling. Give her a feeling of what your life is like away from her. And every once in a while (at least once per page), name something that you miss about her. It can be a simple phrase in the middle of a sentence or a separate paragraph—but again, be specific. Think of it as interspersing "little love notes" throughout. This keeps the focus on her and lets her know that you truly do think of her.

After you've gone into whatever detail you like with what you've been up to, ask her what she's been doing. Mention how you like to picture her: sitting in her favorite chair with the cat on her lap, raking the leaves, dancing in her lingerie. End with words of love. Tell her you're anxious to be with her again.

And sign off with the sweetest words you have for her.

From one of our survey respondents:

I opened my mailbox and among the bills and junk mail was a beige envelope with my name and address written out lavishly in blue ink. Curious, I opened it right there at the end of the drive. It was from Jack—telling me how much he enjoys being with me. Well, there was more—about his flight, his meetings, etc.—but what I focused on was the fact that he missed me. I stood there and read it over and over again. I have never been more surprised or grateful.

Of course you don't need to be away to write a letter to her. If you have something you want her to know—especially if you have trouble telling her face-to-face or if you want to formalize the message—by all means, write to her.

You may want to apologize for something that's come between you. Leave the letter where she'll find it—maybe next to the flowers you just bought for her.

Maybe you had an argument and you want to clarify your thoughts to her. To do this, outline your thoughts in advance. Explain your understanding of how she feels on the issue and then tell her how you feel about it and why you feel the way you do. According to our survey respondents, too often women are told that they don't understand or can't see reason. Their thoughts and ideas are often overlooked or not given enough serious consideration by men. So be sure you give her credit for her own thoughts on the issue. And let her know that it's not a matter of "you're right" and "she's wrong"; rather, it's a matter of a difference of opinion. The "little love notes" that you intersperse throughout this letter need to be well grounded so as not to sound patronizing or seem frivolous.

But you don't need an excuse to write a love letter any more than you need an excuse to write a little love note. If you would like to let her know how much you care for her—but in a more serious way than a fun little love note—by all means put it into a letter. Tell her about life before her—how empty it was. Tell her how much she's changed your life, your thoughts, your feelings. Mention all those ways that she's special to you. Say things you're afraid to say out loud. And of course intersperse "little love notes" throughout—and make them as intimate as you dare.

Here's a sample. Not too long. Nothing important to say. But it lets a woman know that her partner cares:

My Dearest Celia,

   Thinking of you now as I lie lonely on this big hotel bed with the couple in the next room crying out . . . makes me think of you . . . and it's driving me wild.

   Arrived yesterday. Beautiful city, much to see, but no fun without you. That moon up there is shining over you right now—do you see it?

   Productive meetings. Presentation went well. I think I impressed them all. Maynard gave hints of a promotion if this thing goes through. It'll be a lot of overtime to get it right— yes, but just temporary. And now that I'm set up at home, I can work with you at my side. Dear Celia, I do appreciate your help and understanding.

*And how are things going with James? Did you finish the
report? I'm sure it will be well received. You're so creative.
You're the one who deserves the promotion.*

*Found a great novel at the bookstore today. I should be
working on the follow-up notes for tomorrow, but just now I
need a break. You'll love this story. I want to discuss it with
you as soon as you read it.*

*Michael . . . Sarah . . . give them hugs for me. Such a ter-
rific mother you are.*
I dream of you!
All my love . . .
    Mitch

Another way to write a love letter is in a journal style. If
you're in the habit of keeping a journal, this may be the most
comfortable method for you—whether or not you're away
from your partner.

Tuesday, 10:47 pm
Darling
    *Thinking of you here in this cold hotel room. Things did
not go so well at the exhibit today . . . and I know that if
only you were here I could disappear into your soft skin
and forget this awful trip.*

Thursday, 9:30 pm
    *Just put the finishing touches on my presentation. Hopeful
after my meeting yesterday with the partners. Keep your
fingers crossed. Now to bed . . . to dream of you.*

Friday, 2 pm
    *Yes! It worked. We hit it off and they'll be coming back
to the office next month to sign the papers. And finally, I'm
on my way back home to you!*
All my love—
    Sammy

Love Implements

Use stick-ums if you like. Anything that conveys your love message will be appreciated. So if you don't like to spend too much time on the details, skip this section. But if you want to really do it right, here's how.

Begin with the stationery. It's not expensive. You can find it at a department store, stationery store, or even your corner drugstore. You'll usually find it near the greeting cards. Choose a color that says "you" but that will also be pleasing to your partner—such as eggshell, peach, or blue—to provide a pleasing background for your message. Or you might want to look for something unique, such as handmade or parchment paper.

For short love notes, you'll want to get something called "personal stationery," which is five by seven inches. For a short love note, you can use a blank greeting card, i.e., the kind with a photo or illustration on the front and a blank interior. But please don't use a regular greeting card with somebody else's message already written in it. That is *not* romantic.

For longer letters, buy 8½-by-11-inch paper. Be sure to purchase matching envelopes if they're not already included with the stationery.

If you plan a trip, remember to pack stationery and stamps. If you've forgotten, check your hotel room for a folder of stationery or ask the concierge if you could have a few pages of the hotel's letterhead and envelopes. If nothing else, at least send a postcard (but see section on postcards later in this chapter).

Activities to Hone Your Romantic Spirit

- Make a list of all the little things you can intersperse throughout your love letters to your partner: I miss (whatever is appropriate); I love your (whatever); you do (something special) for me; I need you; I'm thinking of you even now; etc. Try to be creative, but more importantly, be honest.

- Practice writing a love letter to your partner on notebook paper. Leave space between the lines and in the margins for inserts. Start by writing a paragraph about what you're doing today—at home, at work, out and about. Then add a paragraph about what you want to accomplish tomorrow. Now add a third paragraph about your life in general—how you feel about it, where it's going, how it's been, whatever. Now go back and insert a few lines into the first paragraph about how you enjoy your partner's company—mention something specific: what she did for you yesterday, how you appreciate her listening to you, what a great time you had last night, whatever. Then insert at least one sentence into each of the following paragraphs, telling her that you're thinking of her. Write a final paragraph about your appreciation of your relationship. And sign off with the most loving closing you can muster. Use a nickname if you dare.
- On nice paper, rewrite (or type) the letter you practiced in Activity #2 and send it to her in the mail.
- If you go away on a trip, be sure to write. Even if you know the letter will arrive after you return home.
- When she travels away from you, write to her—either to her travel address (if she'll be there long enough to receive it) or to her home address for her to find upon her return.
- If you have an argument, or if you know that you've disappointed her, write down your feelings. Intersperse "little love notes" about how you need her.
- If she accomplishes something special, write her a congratulatory letter.
- Go to your local department store, stationery store, or drugstore and choose appropriate stationery or blank cards.
- While you're at the stationery store, try out a variety of pens before settling on the one that you will use in your love letters. And if want to go totally romantic, check out the sealing wax.

- Go to the post office and take a look at the variety of stamps available. Choose one that says "love"—whether it's a heart, the word "love," or a design depicting something that you share in love with her. Buy a roll of them.
- If you're handy with a computer and feel comfortable about design—whether or not you use a computer for the body of the letter—you could fashion yourself a masthead or logo (i.e., your name or initials across the top of the page). If you do have a masthead printed on your stationery, use it for only the first page of the letter; subsequent pages should be written on blank paper.

Formalizing Special Occasions

Certain occasions call for a special kind of correspondence. When such occasions arise—when you plan a special occasion for her or when she has done something special for you—invitations and thank you notes bring messages she's sure to appreciate.

The Invitation

Whether it's for a formal dinner and dance or a fun little picnic, if you want to add a special touch to an invitation, put it in writing and mail it to her.

You can use small stationery for an invitation, or you can purchase blank cards for this purpose. But even a blank piece of paper or a note card will do. The message can be typed or written out longhand.

Formal invitations are centered on the page and often written in the third person ("she" and "he" rather than "you" and "I"). But of course pet names and private language add to the fun.

The following is an example of an invitation to a special event:

Mr. Martin. P. Ballard
requests the pleasure of
Mrs. Christine D. Ballard
at the evening performance of Sleeping Beauty
Friday, the first of March
at 8 o'clock
The Ballet Theater
R.S.V.P.

A whimsical touch:

BooBoo Bear
requests the pleasure of your company
at a dinner
to be held at the Stork Restaurant
on the evening of Saturday, the twelfth of November
at seven o'clock
R.S.V.P.

Even a dinner at home can be made more special with a written invitation:

Donny Dearest
requests the pleasure of
Shirley Darling
at home
on the evening of Sunday, the tenth of October
at five o'clock
R.S.V.P.

For an added flair, prepare a written menu to present at the meal:

Billy's Barbecued Chicken Supreme
Foil-Baked Potatoes in Skins
Italian Salad Bowl
Grilled Tomato Slices
Cantaloupe & Ice Cream
Chardonnay

For something less formal, such as an afternoon boating, a picnic, or a little "escape" luncheon in the middle of the week:

My Dearest Martha,
   Will you lunch with me on Tuesday the seventh of April at half past twelve o'clock? In hopes that you will, I have taken the liberty of making reservations at your favorite bistro—Gerard's.
Do say yes!
Love,
   Tod

The Thank You Note

Of course you thank her when she does something special for you. But why not do it in a special way? Write the message out longhand. Be specific about the reason for the thank you. Then, in a second "paragraph," add something that speaks of your appreciation in more personal terms.

Dearest Mary,
Thank you, my sweet, for revising my résumé—I look better on paper now than I do in reality.
You are always there for me—and I appreciate it.
Love,
   Sam

It's also romantic to send a little note of appreciation for no reason except that you're glad she's with you:

Darling,
You do so much for me . . . thanks for just being there . . .
Love,
   Alex

And Everything in Between

Anytime, and from wherever you are—home or away—love messages can create fun and surprise.

The Postcard

If you find yourself traveling without your stationery, by all means, pick up a postcard. If you can, find a photo that carries a special meaning for your relationship (that's much more romantic than just a photo of the motel pool).

A simple little message is all you need: a few words about what you've been doing, how much you miss her, and how you're anxious to see her again.

Dear Maria,
Long uneventful flight. Meeting went well. Wish I was cuddling with you right now. Be there soon . . . !
Love, R

The Electronic Message

Whether she's in the next room or on the other side of the globe, if you're connected electronically, you can send her fun little messages throughout the day. "Hi Babe, thinking of you . . ." "Hey Gorgeous, I'm bringing home the dinner tonight . . . " "Well Little Lover, get ready 'cause I'm outa here . . . see you in ten . . . !"

And you don't have to stop at the one-minute message. If you're a computer kind of guy, you may feel more comfortable sending longer love letters electronically. Even apologies, thank yous and invitations can be sent electronically.

If it works for you, do it.

Faxing messages can be fun, too, as long as the fax machines on either end are for your and her eyes only—unless you want to try faxing in another language or in code.

Stick-ums, Grocery Lists, and Bill Envelopes

She'll find fun and romance in little love notes that show up in surprising places and unusual circumstances—reminders that you're thinking of her. Here are a few suggestions:

Leave stick-ums with little love messages inside her cupboard doors, on her car dashboard, on her calendar.

Surreptitiously sneak her grocery list before she goes to the
store and add a little "love" item—not something for her to
buy, but something for her to smile about.

Stick a little note into her favorite pair of shoes, reading from
"left" to "right."

Be creative; come up with some of your own. It's always romantic to tell her you're thinking of her, wanting her, impatient
to be with her . . .

Activities to Hone Your Romantic Spirit

- The next time you arrange for a special surprise date, send
  her a formal invitation with an RSVP.
- When you plan a special dinner—a formal white-linen affair
  or a backyard barbecue—send her an invitation. And take
  care of all the preparations: shopping, setting up, cooking,
  and cleaning up afterward.
- After a special evening together, send her a note thanking
  her for being so much fun.
- After she does something special for you, write her a special
  thank you.
- The next time you're traveling without stationery, pick up a
  postcard and send her a little love note. Best if the picture
  has a personal message.
- When you're not traveling, go to your local drugstore and
  pick up a postcard—it's best if it a carries a message that will
  make her smile. Write her a little "missing you" message.
  Put on a stamp and stick it in the mail.
- Hide stick-ums where she's sure to find them—little notes
  that describe various things about her that you love. "I love
  the scent of your hair," "Your eyes have captured me,"
  "Thanks for listening last night," and so on. Whatever it is
  that you truly appreciate about her.

- Write her a poem and send it in the mail. Or write a love song—and sing it to her at a well-chosen moment. (If you're too shy to sing it in person, put it on her answering machine or an audio tape.)
- Send her a typed note saying she has won a trip for two— even if it's just a night for two at the Big Hotel up the highway, whatever you can reasonably afford.
- If you're already communicating via electronic mail, spice it up—add a love note once in a while. Throw in an occasional invitation. Try a longer love letter. If you each work at a computer and you're not yet connected, get connected. Even if you share a home computer, you can still leave little notes for her to find.
- Send her a "junk mail" flier promoting yourself as a primo lover, cook, handyman, whatever it is you *want* to be. Be sure to note that you're sending it to a very elite clientele of one.

6

If She's a Mom

Even the simplest products you bring home from the store come with instructions: "Charge for 24 hours before using." "Store in cool place." "Cold water wash, gentle cycle, do not bleach."

Babies are the most precious package of all. But if a child came with an instruction manual, the basic rules, regulations, and limited warranties would encompass a shelf of encyclopedias. A challenge for anyone.

So why is it that for centuries women have grown healthy children without instruction manuals?

It's because mothering comes naturally—to mothers. And from the day that furry little head peeks out into the world, he or she is Mother's Number One priority—for years to come.

Can you sustain a romantic relationship with a woman who gives the best of her time, energy, and emotional support to her children?

No matter how smart, how capable, how sweet she is, Mom just doesn't have a lot left for romance. It's not that she doesn't want to be romantic. Our survey found many mothers calling for help.

If youngsters—or relatives of any age—live with you and/or your partner, read on. Discussion here is relevant to situations created by the newest little newborn still trying to find his thumb, to that big oaf of a grown "child" who's decided to move back home. Some ideas may also apply to aging parents who have come to live with you. Anyone Mom needs to care for can create enormous demands on her time, energy, and emotions.

According to the mothers who answered our survey, time pressures, work, stress, fatigue, and mostly children get in the way of romance. In analyzing written comments, we see that in order to sustain romance, three interdependent facets of the family structure require nurturing:

- *The family as a whole.* If children of any age are living at home, you must spend time together as a family.
- *The parenting couple.* If you want your romance to last beyond the children's stay at home, you must take "time out" with your partner.
- *The individuals.* To preserve your sanity, you must have time alone. And you must give Mother time alone, as well. The children, too, as they grow, need time away from you and your partner to discover their own individualities.

The needed balance among these facets depends upon the age of the children and the needs of each individual involved. But none can be ignored.

Keep Family Together

Based upon our survey responses, if your partner is a mother, you will have a better chance of enjoying a romantic bond with her if you also create a strong bond with the children.

In talking with family therapists, we have learned that whether or not you and your partner are married—and irrespective of whether the children are yours, hers, or "ours"—if children live at home, you must take time together as a family. Not only will this time investment provide the children with much needed emotional support and encouragement, but it will also allow you and your partner to experience being children again. And if you allow yourself to play, you may even have fun.

It starts when the infant comes home. Bringing that little one into bed with you in the morning can be very romantic—and emotionally rewarding for all three of you. Laugh and talk and coo together. It's the interaction that's so important.

And it continues as you splash together in the wading pool or push the jingle bubble back and forth or make laughing faces at each other.

Our survey respondents had a lot to say about the fathering capabilities of their partners. On one side, we received comments about men who didn't take the time. One example: "Bill's always so anxious about his work, he never hears what the children are trying to tell him—mainly, 'play with me!' He hardly knows them any more."

On the other side were the women who appreciated the family involvement, such as this one:

> One thing about Danny that makes me feel so good about him is the way he relates to the kids. He's always asking Karen if she needs help with her homework—he's really helped her turn her grades around. And he encourages all of us to go out together on weekend hikes and bike rides. I trust and respect him so much as a father.

Learn to Relate

Children have so much to teach us about play. And through play, you can nurture the family relationship. Depending upon the age of the children, you can play blocks or chess. Or make up your own game.

If someone in the family plays a musical instrument, buy some sheet music to familiar tunes and sing along; this is particularly meaningful during important holidays, including birthdays. Speaking of which, when it comes time for your partner's birthday or Mother's Day, be sure to involve the children in the arrangements, which might include cake baking, shopping, or wrapping. Mom will love it.

To find out what to do with children in your local area, go to your city library or bookstore, or call your town newspaper and ask if they have a guide to places and activities. The front pages of your phone book may have a map noting parks and points of interest to visit. Who knows, a hidden museum may be within walking distance of your home.

If you can afford it, take the family off together someplace with no radio or TV—a cabin on the lake or a camping trip in the mountains—and get to know each other. And learn who you really are, as a family. This just might be as good for you as it will be for the rest of the family.

As an alternative, find a family camp. The YMCA and Sierra Club are two of many organizations that offer such vacations. Again, your local library should be of help in finding sources.

Or if you've got great friends with children of ages similar to yours, try taking a vacation with them. That way you'll be with adults you enjoy and your youngsters will have friends to play with as well.

Another idea is to take vacations at places that provide child care and teen activities. That way, you can spend time together as a family, and you can also take time out to relax alone with your partner knowing that your children are having fun on their own. Check out major hotels, cruise ships, and clubs. Club Med offers special baby care at some of their resorts and supervised teen activities at others. A good travel agent will be able to advise you.

One of our survey respondents told us about an organization called TWYCH (Travel with Your Children), which offers a newsletter with information about where to vacation with your children, including reviews of sites and activities. You can reach TWYCH at 45 West 18th Street, New York, New York, 10011, phone 212/206-0688.

Include Teens

Teenagers are often the hardest to include because they just don't want to be included. If you start when they're young, they'll expect to take part in the family vacation. But if you're starting from scratch with a teenager, you may need to do some cajoling before bringing up that trip across country in the rented trailer or the escape to the quiet lake without radios or TVs.

Try to get involved in your teenager's activities long before you spring this one on him or her. Even if staring at the boob tube and talking on the telephone are the only activities your teen ever engages in, take advantage of it. For example, special TV shows and movies can bring up controversial subjects for discussion.

Then start inviting your teenager on little excursions you think he or she will enjoy; she might not want to go to the company picnic with you (unless of course she can invite her boyfriend with the ponytail and earring in his nose), but she may take you up on a trip to her favorite clothing store (especially if you happen to find an extra $20 you might just share with her).

If you're having a great deal of trouble dealing with your teen, try joining a Tough Love group in your area (for information, write to Tough Love, P.O. Box 1069, Doylestown, Pennsylvania 18901). Your local high school may also be helpful in making recommendations.

When you do get away to "family" together, remember that it's ok for you to spend at least some of your time apart. If you like to play tennis and your partner would rather be in aerobics and the children have supervision in the pool, separate for a few hours. And then when you meet for lunch, compare notes.

Whatever you do, wherever you go—keep in touch as a family. Touch, hug, talk, listen. And appreciate the love that comes in return.

Activities to Hone Your Romantic Spirit

Following are examples of actions and activities which, according to our survey respondents, express the romantic spirit. Try one or two now, and then come back later for more when you feel comfortable enough to take a few more risks.

- Bring the family together in an activity you can all share. If the family members don't generally do anything together, watch activities enjoyed by the individuals and determine what they might all enjoy as a group.
- Involve the youngsters in some activity that you generally perform yourself: cooking, cleaning the garage, washing the car, walking the dog, whatever. Be patient. Maybe they can teach *you* a thing or two.
- Involve the youngsters in a surprise celebration for your partner: her birthday, Mother's Day, Valentine's Day. Or make something up. Get them involved in the planning and preparation, and then surprise your lady love. (If the children are old enough, let them carry the card or the cake or the breakfast tray.)
- Consult a travel agent to find out about vacations your family can take together and places that provide activities for youngsters the ages of yours. Bring brochures home and discuss the trip with your partner—and then the family.
- You may be disappointed at some of your efforts to bring the family together. Don't give up. Ask your partner for help. And keep trying.

Steal Away Together

Women with children rated the statement "He treats me as the most special person in his life" as one of two top priorities on our survey. Mothers spend so much time making life special for their families that they need to know they are Number One with you.

Plan Quiet Time

It's important to let the children know that you and your partner need to spend quiet time together. For starters, set aside a time—at least half an hour—each day when you and that busy mother can talk alone together. Maybe it's before the children wake in the morning or after they go to sleep at night. If you both work, you might want to meet for lunch. Or if a trustworthy baby-sitter is handy, have the baby-sitter take the children out to the park each day. Whatever you decide, put it on your calendar and make it a priority in your schedule. It will probably be the most important meeting of your day.

If the children are old enough to play without supervision, teach them that you need time alone together. Lock your door if you must; they may balk at first, but after a while they'll get the message that this is serious. Put on your answering machine and instruct your children not to answer the phone during this time (unless they're old enough to take a message so that you can return the call later). Talk about dreams, plans, mutual concerns. Or take advantage of this time to make love. But make sure it's a quiet time that won't be interrupted.

Take one night a week to feed the children and put them to bed early (if they're young enough) or send them off to play (if they're old enough) so that you can have a late leisurely dinner together. You might even think of trading evenings or overnights with a neighbor who has children of similar ages.

Make a Date

Unless you have a new baby, plan at least one evening a week when the two of you can go out and have fun the way you used to. It doesn't have to be expensive. Go out to dinner, to a bookstore, to a high-school basketball game. Sign up for a class you would both enjoy. If nothing else, at least get carryouts and rent a good movie to watch after the children are in bed.

Survey respondents with children rated as one of their highest romantic priorities "He arranges for us to have time alone together."

Remember how to flirt? Become lovers again. When you're looking forward to a scheduled "date," remind her about it with little looks, kisses, and touches as the days get closer. Let her know that you just can't wait to be with her alone again. Let her know that her special charm enchants you still. Give yourself permission to fall in love with her again and again and again.

One survey respondent told us the results of her special time away:

> I love to dance, but after Jeremy was born, it was difficult to think of leaving him. When he was about eight months old, we found a terrific baby-sitter who agreed to come and stay with him every Saturday night. Once we started dancing on a regular basis, the romance came back into our marriage. And the exercise helped me get back into shape—and I started feeling sexy again.

Another young mother told us:

> We couldn't afford much after the twins came, but Jerry insisted that we go to a nice restaurant at least once a month. It helped sustain my sanity—as well as our marriage—during those exhausting years.

And yet a third showed us a bit of ingenuity in planning time together for a weekly brunch.

> The mall in our town has a child-care facility for shoppers. And they also have a great place for omelets. So each Sunday morning after church we drive to the mall and drop off Jody at the child-care center. He has fun with the other children while the two of us find each other again.

Use the time alone together to regain your personal energy and reestablish that wonderful relationship that once was. Use it to revisit the delights of each other's bodies. You can also use this time away from the children to discuss concerns about their needs and behaviors. Children will cope much better in a family where the two parents agree on the rules and relationships.

Get Away

Take her away. Alone? you ask.

Yes. It's ok to take time away from your children. In fact, according to responses from our survey, in order to sustain your love relationship, you *must* take time together away from the children. This usually means rearranging your schedules to make time for each other. It means making sure that the children are properly and lovingly cared for while you are away—even if it's just for an afternoon. In other words, it takes planning.

Keeping your relationship vital is something you *choose* to do. If you're sacrificing your love relationship for your children, you're probably making yourself—and the kids—miserable.

The most common romantic fantasy of women with children was a weekend or week away without the children, arranged by their partner.

As one survey respondent put it:

> I wish my husband and I had invested more time and money in our love relationship. The divorce was much more expensive—and much more traumatic for the children than occasional weekends away would have been!

But be sure to take the age of the children into consideration. If you and Mom have any doubts about whether Johnny and Susie are old enough to be left with a sitter, speak with their pediatrician.

You can make this time special for children, as well. One mother told us that she and her husband brought their son a library book or bought him a small toy each time they planned to leave him for an overnight trip. Another made sure her children had special treats. And a third arranged play times with friends so that her daughter would have fun and maintain comfortable relationships while Mom and Dad were away.

Having trouble finding a good baby-sitter? If your partner doesn't already have a stable of good sitters, start by asking other parents for references. Talk with your child's day-care or nursery school. Speak with your priest or rabbi or with other parents in your church or synagogue. Check with your local high school for references. Ask people at your office. Ask your neighbors—you may find a responsible teenager or "grandparent" not far from your own neighborhood.

One woman wrote to tell us of her plan for getaway success:

> I'm great friends with a woman in my office who has two children about the same age as mine. They love to play together. So it seemed natural for us to trade baby-sitting. I take her children one weekend, and she takes mine the next. It's grand for all of us, and it doesn't cost us a thing.

Plan a Great Escape

Once the children are old enough, plan an overnight trip away—even if it's just to the motel across town. If this is new to you, start with something small. If you live in a large city, get tickets to a play or a symphony. Even in a small town you can find entertaining musicals or sporting events at the local high school or community center.

Later, plan a weekend away together. Even the planning can be romantic. Revisit the place where you met. Or just take a drive to the country—or to the city. Get away from your normal routine to rejuvenate your relationship.

Once you've found someone reliable to care for your youngsters, and your partner is satisfied that she can take off without worry, it's time for *you* to take the initiative to arrange for outings and weekends. Surprise her. Bring home tickets to a night on the town, a weekend away, or—if a reliable baby-sitter, relative, or neighbor can keep the children at his or her home for a night or two—surprise your partner with an evening home alone. Get creative. Bring home roses, candlelight, and dinner.

One appreciative woman shared her experience:

> One Friday night he came home and told me that we were going out to dinner. The two little ones were at his parents for the weekend. He had arranged it all. The place was ours. And we could come and go as we pleased. On Saturday we went biking, we went out for a movie, we stayed up late in front of the fire . . . I felt so free! On Sunday morning we lounged in bed and later made waffles together. His parents had a wonderful time with the children (and vice versa), so now this is a regular event.

Another mother wrote to tell us of a wonderful day of hooky. She and her husband took an impromptu day of vacation from work and just "played around" while the children were in school.

When children are old enough, help them find entertainment with friends away from home (teen clubs, recreation centers, athletic lessons)—for their own sake as well as for yours.

Most children enjoy going away to camp. When your children are old enough, find a reputable weekend or week-long camp that offers activities that interest them. If you don't know of one, check with your local community center, the YMCA, or your church or synagogue. A travel agent may help. Or call a camp agent (see your Yellow Pages). Take advantage of the time while children are away by either staying home with your partner or taking a vacation yourselves. Break out of your routine. Your relationship has grown and changed over the years, and now it's time to mark how good this new phase is.

Activities to Hone Your Romantic Spirit

- As soon as you arrive home, find her and give her a hug. And hug the children, too. And if you don't already practice touching her in *nonsexual* ways, do it now, in front of the children.
- Give her a compliment about the way she looks (she really needs this now). Be truthful and specific.

- Flirt! Pinch her thigh under the table. Blow her a kiss across the nursery. Sneak up and nuzzle her on the neck when she's folding the laundry. Laugh and wink and sing little ditties and let her know you still think she's a very sexy lady.
- Discuss with your partner the need to schedule a time alone together each day, and plan how that will happen. Then hold her to it.
- Take responsibility for finding a reliable baby-sitter. When you go out, provide a detailed checklist of what the children need in terms of routines, schedules, food, and toys. Explain house rules, including cleanup, phone use, snacks allowed (for children and sitter), rooms where food is allowed, and whether or not the sitter can have guests while you're away from the house. Leave phone numbers to call in case of emergency: where you will be (to be used for emergencies only, please) as well as your children's doctors, your neighbors, and any close relatives. Let the sitter know what to do in case of emergencies in the home (e.g., if the electricity goes out). And be sure to call and let the sitter know if your plans change—if you will be at a different phone number or if you will be delayed in returning home.
- If you have pets, be sure to arrange for pet care, as well.
- When she least expects it, tell your partner how much you desire her and that you can't wait to be alone with her.
- If the children are old enough and if you have proper care for them, plan a "great escape"—a night or weekend or week away alone with your lady love.
- If the children are older, look into sending them off to a reputable camp where they can learn and have fun, too. At the same time, plan time alone with your partner—either at home or away.

Give Her a Break

Parenting is filled with inexplicable joy. Watching a youngster learn and grow and laugh and cry can bring emotions that transcend all others. Seeing your own reflection in your child's looks or abilities can renew your belief in immortality.

But what about romance? Even if you've played and escaped and done all those other romantic things you needed to do to keep everybody happy, those everyday problems still appear on the scene. Youngsters need lots of attention, to be sure. Much of it is loving assurance, much of it is teaching, and much of it is "playing it by ear." As they grow older, children test the boundaries—and they always seem to know just when you're most vulnerable.

You arrive home ready for a wonderful evening with that terrific woman you love and find that Bobby's crying because his truck lost a wheel and Megan wants Mom to help her with homework and Sarah's running a fever. Maybe Mom's coping well, or maybe she's not. But she is definitely not available for you.

If you're a father, or if you're dating a woman with children, you're probably thinking, "Sure, I'd love to just hold her and be romantic . . . but you've gotta be kidding. That's the last thing she has on her mind!"

Where did that romantic woman go?

In answer to a survey question "Has any one thing dramatically changed your relationship for better or for worse," again and again the answer from mothers was "children." Unfortunately, most mothers wrote that children were a major factor in draining romance *out* of the relationship. As much as mothers love their children, the demands of those little ones (and the big ones, too) sap women of time and energy—time and energy she may have once given to you.

As one frustrated mother wrote:

I've got a teenage son. I guess that says it all. But I'll add that I love him and I'll add again that he's a real manipulator. He always springs the hard ones on me when I'm stressed and in a rush— rushing off to work in the morning, getting ready for a date on a Saturday night, or calling me at work in the middle of a meeting. It usually goes something like this: "Hey Mom, how's it goin'? Everybody's goin' over to Josh's tonight and so I won't be home until Sunday sometime ok? And we'll probably be off at that dancing place so don't try to call or anything. I mean everybody's going to be there. I gotta go. Pat's waiting to use the phone. I gotta ride. Ok? Thanks Mom. See ya' Sunday. Have a good weekend." He's 15.

At one time a mother had an extended family to support her. But today—with our transient culture and our expectations for women to do everything they once did while, at the same time, contributing to the financial well-being of the family—women are literally going crazy. Today's society tells women they should be able to do it all: perform well in a fulfilling career, maintain a clean home, serve nourishing meals, keep themselves beautiful, grow smart and happy children . . . and yes, sustain a meaningful love relationship. Something's gotta give! And more often than not, we learned, it's the relationship.

Statistics show that if you have youngsters in your home, your partner is exhausted—whether she works outside the home or spends her days with the children. If her day is at all typical, she takes care of the meals (planning, shopping, cooking, cleaning up afterward); she is the children's chauffeur (scouts, Little League, doctor appointments, school activities); she is the comforter when the children are sick; and she is ultimately responsible for making sure that everything is neat and tidy. She may also take responsibility for other general household chores such as paying the bills, running the errands, and . . . you know there's more. All the while the children are tugging at her for attention.

If this woman is the woman you love, you hopefully take on a good part of the burden. Many a woman wrote, however, that even if her partner played an equal role in performing household chores *before* the baby was born, the additional chores *after* the baby came fell to the mother.

The bottom line: She has very little left to give.

We heard from a number of women who felt that the men in their lives didn't allow enough time for the family. But others told us of their appreciation when husbands and boyfriends pitched in. Here's an example:

> Fred's great with the kids. They can't wait to see him when he comes home. He gets down on the floor and plays with them. He hugs them and jounces them around. He tells them funny stories that they probably don't even understand yet, but they laugh. It's terrific for me, too, because I know that when he comes home from work, I can take time to recharge. He's a real partner in this relationship and we're making a great family.

How can you help bring out all that sexy loving stuff that this woman is capable of? You know it's in there, just waiting for the time when she can turn her energies again to you. Please don't make her wait until the children have left home—so many wasted years. Start right now. Read on. And save your romance.

Give Her Time Off

Everyone needs time alone to think and regain mental and emotional strength. But most mothers feel guilty about time taken away from their families. If they're not at work or out with their partners, they'd better be with their children.

You need time off. And hopefully you're taking care of yourself. But she needs time off, too. So give her a break. Literally. Even an hour or two can enhance her outlook on life, renew her energy, and help her feel less trapped.

While she's recouping her energy, you can take advantage of your time alone with the children. Get to know them. Teach them to play Go Fish or Monopoly—and let them win once in a while. Forget about your own cares. And have fun.

A single mom offered this:

When past boyfriends came to pick me up for a date, well, I used to be frantic because I was never ready. But Tom's different. Now I can't wait for him to arrive. He comes in and takes over. He's great with the kids. He plays with them; he makes them laugh. He gives me time to cool down and start thinking about our evening ahead. I take a shower, perfume my hair, and by the time I'm dressed to go out—or stay in—I want only to be with him. Sometimes he even puts the kids to bed and reads to them until they fall asleep and we've got the house to ourselves. They're not his kids, but he makes me feel I'm not shouldering everything myself. I've got support. And I let him know that I appreciate everything he does!

Depending upon the youngsters' ages, you can read them a story, throw a baseball around, show them how to play hoops or Gin Rummy. Help them with their homework. Explain the ball game on TV. Jog alongside their bikes. Or teach them how to ride a bike. Seek out community activities in your area. Sign up for scheduled lessons with them at your community center—tennis, volleyball, swimming. If you belong to a gym, take them along. Teach them to dance. Go fly a kite.

Help Her Relax

There are other ways to help your partner relax as well.

If your partner makes dinner for the family every night, suggest that she not worry about preparing dinner by a certain time every night. Give her time to relax first—by herself or with the family.

After dinner, offer to clean up the dishes or get the children to bed so that she can take a bath or read a book or "slip into something more comfortable."

And if you're not in the habit of making dinner for the family yourself, try it—you might like it. Involve the children if they're old enough. If cooking dinner seems beyond your capability, pick up carryouts—something that the whole family can enjoy. And whatever you do, be sure to clean up the kitchen afterward.

One day after work when she comes home exhausted or when you arrive to find her frantic, suggest that she take some time out—on her own—while you take care of things. Suggest that she take a long bath, or take the newspaper and a cup of coffee or a glass of wine out to the back porch, or go for a walk, or ride her bike, or go shopping . . . whatever she enjoys doing.

A few weeks later, do it again. And eventually work this up into a standard arrangement—maybe every week. Create a schedule with her so that she can plan her evenings out, either alone or with her friends.

The morning can be just as demanding as the evening. If she's in the habit of making everyone's breakfast and getting children ready for school, surprise her with an offer to take over one day. Let *her* sleep in.

On weekend mornings, take turns getting up early to diaper the baby or take Chris to Little League or Jenny to gymnastics. And if you're good in the kitchen (or if you've thought ahead and made that side trip to the local bakery), surprise her with her favorite breakfast—in or out of bed (whichever *she* prefers). Add a pretty napkin, the Sunday paper, and a fresh flower for good measure.

Maybe she wants to take a good book to brunch alone on a Sunday morning. Why not, if this is what will rejuvenate her? Suggest it. Or help her find a few hours of free time on a Saturday or Sunday afternoon. You'll see how much more relaxed she is when she returns home.

In any case, make sure that your partner does *not* use this time for grocery shopping or cleaning the closets. This "time out" is meant to help her recoup some of that energy, some of those good feelings about herself, about her life, and toward you. Give her a gift certificate for a professional massage, a manicure, or shopping at her favorite clothing store. And give her the time to take advantage of it.

If your partner stays home with small children during the day, suggest that she hire a teenager to come in after school on a regular basis—a few times a week, for example—to do some household chores or make the children's dinner so that she can relax and take time for herself—even if that only means a leisurely walk. If she works, suggest that she hire a teenager occasionally for a few hours on a Saturday or Sunday afternoon (or trade with a neighbor) so that you can each do your own thing—and return to each other refreshed.

When the children are old enough, make sure they do their part in keeping the household running smoothly—for their sake as well as Mom's. Talk with your partner about setting out daily schedules of chores and responsibilities for the youngsters. Start with simple things, such as clearing the dishes off the dinner table, and eventually move up to taking responsibility for keeping the kitchen clean—as well as their own rooms. Young teenagers should be able to do their own laundry, take care of a pet, and help clean the garage. The children's pediatrician is a good resource for determining age-appropriate capabilities.

Activities to Hone Your Romantic Spirit

- Ask her about her day. Listen listen listen to her daily problems and travails. Don't think you have to come up with answers to problems. For now, just let her know that you love her and support her.
- Every day tell your partner something positive about herself—about the way she looks, or what she accomplishes at work or home, or why you love her. Start right now. Do it in front of the children whenever you can.
- Practice saying, "Relax . . . I'll take care of it." Now say it again . . . and again . . . and now say it in front of her. See, that wasn't so bad.
- Surprise her. Leave work early one evening and arrive home with the makings of a terrific dinner—early, before she has time to start anything. (If you can't cook, bring home carryouts from a good deli; or if you're feeling flush, hire a caterer.) Light candles. Turn on her favorite music, start a

fire going in the fireplace, put a rose on the table—whatever is appropriate to make a romantic scene. If you can, pick up the kids from day-care and have them all clean, fed, and happy by the time she gets home (you might want to bring in their favorite baby-sitter to help). Make your partner's arrival a special event and serve her royally.

- If you're living with small children in the house, make a point of taking your turn at least a couple days a week to get up early and get the children fed and dressed and ready for the day ahead.

- Give her a compliment about the way she mothers—something specific.

- Give her a book of coupons that she can cash in as needed. Offer those things that you feel most comfortable doing and that you know she will appreciate: good for one vacuuming. . . . kitchen patrol . . . dinner preparation . . . baby diapering . . . breakfast in bed . . . chauffeuring . . . homework hour with Tommy . . . grocery shopping . . . car washing . . . reading to the children . . . gardening . . . and so forth. If the children are old enough, enlist their help.

- If you don't already participate in mealtime activities, take over either the dinner shopping and meal preparation or the cleaning up afterward—on a regular basis. If she doesn't want you in the kitchen, at least offer to care for the children while she does the cooking.

- On a weekend morning or afternoon, offer to take care of the children while your partner goes off to pursue her own interests: riding her bike, shopping, or maybe just going out for breakfast with the newspaper.

- One day when you arrive to find your partner in the midst of chaos, immediately offer to relieve her. Pick up the crying baby, stir the oatmeal, put out the dog, and tell your overworked lover to go upstairs and soak in a warm bath or retire to the den to read a novel or watch the evening news. Then put on some soothing music, feed the children, comfort them until they're happy (take them for a walk, read to them, give them a bath, whatever they need . . .). And when all is peaceful, go find your Cinderella and hand her a glass of wine or cup of tea to sip while you prepare her dinner.

- Give her a gift certificate for a day at the spa—massage, aromatic therapy, facial, manicure, pedicure, etc. If you are not aware of such services in your area, do a little research. Ask the women in your office or check the Yellow Pages.

7

Occasions, Gifts, and Such

When it comes to gifts and celebrations, women surveyed told us that men are often at a loss. One unfortunate woman told us about a man who was so dumbfounded about gift-giving that he would skip occasions altogether, only later to apologize with "I didn't know what you'd like." Just as sad was the story from the woman who had been handed a check on her birthday to go buy her own present. We also heard stories about men who had someone else do the shopping for their partner's gifts.

Do expensive gifts make women happy? According to the women who responded to our survey, the answer is a resounding no. If you think that the purpose of a gift is to simply spend a lot of money on a woman, you're wrong. The fact is, most western women today are perfectly capable of buying whatever they need.

But if you forget an occasion that she considers special, you'll be in the dog house for sure.

Women have told us that they want *romantic* gifts on special occasions. Gifts that a partner has chosen himself, based upon his knowledge of her.

What are romantic gifts? The best gifts are those things that play to a woman's fantasies. Special things she might not buy for herself because they would be too extravagant, extraneous, or simply vain.

For a woman, romantic gifts are personal gifts—things that adorn her, bring out her beauty, enliven her senses. Giving a woman tire chains for her car because you are concerned for her safety may be thoughtful, but it is not romantic. On the other hand, even the smallest gift, if presented in a loving and imaginative way, can be very romantic.

The perfect gift shows your partner that you have paid enough attention to her to know what pleases her and that you are willing to do something special for her. The "gifts" women told us they truly cherish involve time, attention, and special treatment.

From one of our survey respondents:

> The best gift-giver I ever knew would bring me small presents for no reason. His gifts were both stylish and personal. There was a luscious pleated silk scarf, for example, which when it unfolded as it moved on me, opened sensuously into black and rose centers. I would not have bought this scarf for myself because—though I spend a fair amount on my clothes—I'm so practical and this isn't the sort of thing I would wear often enough to warrant the expense. But whenever I did wear it, I felt so sensual. Sometimes I wore it for him—with nothing else . . .

And from another:

> He left to go to the dump with all of our piled-up yard clippings. When he returned, he said, "Hold out your hands." I thought, "Uh-oh, what did he bring back from the dump . . . ?" But to my delight, he presented me with 100 roses (yes, 100!). "Just because I love you," he said.

But don't let these practiced romantics intimidate you. Even the smallest token of love—when given with love—is truly appreciated.

Gifts That Please

When asked what kind of gifts they liked to receive, our respondents had lots to say.

The key to successful gift-giving is knowing what your partner would like. Chapter 10, "Your Romance Notebook," will help you decipher her desires. But in the meantime, observe what she lingers over—or comments upon—in a magazine, catalog, or when you're out together window-shopping. If you do this on a regular basis, you won't be at a loss when the gift-giving time is nigh. Take note of her responses. Remember them for the next occasion. If it's a small thing, give it to her now, for no reason—complete surprise. How romantic!

In fact, although many of the women in our survey rated gifts as a form of romance as low, the majority of them placed a high priority on "small tokens of affection that show me that he thinks of me." A little something hidden in her drawer or under her pillow will make a big impression. "Found" gifts can be especially meaningful. As one survey respondent told us:

> We've been married for 35 years now, and he knows that I enjoy nature. So he often suggests that we go for a walk along the lake. And while we're walking, he finds little gifts for me. He knows me well. In the autumn, he can find the perfect red maple leaf. In the spring, he picks me the first blossom. In the summer, it's strawberries. In the winter, he collects firewood. All these things he presents as gifts. And I accept them as such. And from the autumn leaf to the firelight, I cherish them all.

Small and simple. But the message is clear. He cared enough to go out of his way to remind her of his love.

If you know there is something special she wants and you can surprise her with it, that will be romantic indeed. As one of our survey respondents wrote:

> One year for my birthday my husband gave me a ceramic box and ribbon. It was a very attractive piece on its own, but when I opened the lid, I also found a gold chain necklace. Many months later, I happened to open the box while I was dusting. To my utter surprise was a gold heart to wear on the chain! When my husband

came home, *he* got a big surprise as well. Over the years, he has left little treasures in my box for me to find.

And from another:

I walked out to my car to drive home after a bad day at the office. I started the engine and looked up—to find a beautiful fresh flower underneath my windshield with a note that said, "I love you!"

Surprise her now and again with some token of your affection, and you're showing your romantic spirit.

If your partner is single, take note. Single women told us that they want gifts of the heart, such as commitment, fidelity, and affection. "Love, it's the only gift that counts," wrote one young single woman.

Flowers Are Most Romantic

Flowers were ranked as a definite winner by the women in our survey.

Flowers are nice for Valentine's Day. And they come as a welcome surprise when you both have something out of the ordinary to celebrate, such as a job promotion, the birth of your child, or any other special success. Most importantly, flowers are a favorite gift among women when they appear for no special reason other than to remind her that you are thinking of her.

Flowers can be accompanied by a comment or short note of endearment, such as "To my blossom," or simply, "Thinking of you."

You can surprise her by sending an arrangement to her home or office. (Many of our survey respondents mentioned the joy of receiving flowers at the office and having coworkers "oh" and "ah" and tell them how lucky they were to have such a thoughtful guy. Lots of mileage in this one.)

You can pick up a bouquet at the corner flower stand, at the florist, or even at the grocery store, and deliver it to her in person.

Or you can let her find it when you're not around. How about a single blossom in a bud vase hidden in the refrigerator or placed on her dresser or nightstand or simply laid on her pillow?

Notes Tell a Love Story

Women also ranked love notes very high in the romantic gift department—particularly when they are personally written. Love notes can arrive in her mailbox at home, at work (marked "Personal," of course), or they can appear taped to her bathroom mirror or in her jewelry box.

Love notes can vary from a simple "I love you" on a Post-it left inside her medicine cabinet to a romantic hand-written message on a card sent in the mail. If you have a little love poem budding inside you, get it down on paper and leave it tucked in her panties.

If you haven't written anything but your signature lately, take heart. Anyone can do it. For ideas, see Chapter 5, "Love Notes."

Jewelry Adds Sparkle

Jewelry rated quite high with most women, single and married. The longer a woman has been married, it seems, the more interested she is in receiving jewelry.

The pieces of jewelry most cherished carried special meaning. As one of our younger survey respondents wrote:

We had been dating for a few months when Christmas came around. He seemed pretty nervous when he handed me the box. It contained a chain with a gold locket in the shape of a heart. Of course I immediately put his photo into the locket, and now I wear it always.

Intimidated at the thought of buying jewelry? Start paying attention to what your partner wears, and build on that. What are her favorite colors? Look for earrings, pins, and rings in those colors. What metals does she wear best—silver, gold? Stones—jade, onyx, lapis? How about jewels—sapphire, emerald, ruby?

One of our survey respondents told us that her husband takes her into jewelry stores, "just in case." And sometimes she receives something that had caught her eye.

And from another:

> My husband shows me jewelry ads in catalogs and asks me what I like. And when the time comes for my birthday or other occasion, I often find one of the pieces I admired. I never know which it will be, though, or when, or even if ever. So it always comes as a great surprise. Also, he wraps things in boxes that disguise it—my favorite gold bracelet came in a light-bulb box!

Tickets Will Take Her

Tickets to a performance she would like to attend, especially when you are eager to escort her, is another romantic winner for women of all ages.

One sure-to-please gift is a surprise outing for an evening, day, weekend, or week, in which you do all the planning.

> We were married for about five years and had two children. We never had money or time to do anything. He is very practical, so he would generally give me something I had said we needed—a toaster, a new vacuum, or some other appliance. Not very romantic. But when my birthday came around that year, all he gave me was an envelope. It contained two tickets to the symphony with a note about reservations for dinner at my favorite restaurant. I was thrilled. Not only did he pay attention to what I would enjoy doing (I listen to classical music on the radio), but he wanted to spend the time there with me. It was the most romantic gift he had ever given me.

For a fabulous gift, give her the vacation she's always wanted. Bring your camera. And delight in this special time together, for she will never forget it.

See Chapter 8, "Great Dates," for ideas and suggestions.

Lingerie Can Spark or Sputter

In the lingerie department, women loved it, hated it, and felt everything in between. If you know where she shops and you know her intimate size and what flatters her figure, go ahead and wrap it up.

Does she have a favorite lingerie store? There, you may find someone to help you out. But know her styles, her sizes, and be able to describe her figure. Or bring along a piece of lingerie she recently purchased, which she enjoys wearing.

Does she shop from a catalog? If so, note the things she has ordered and give the catalog company a call for advice.

From one woman:

> One of the most romantic camping trips was when we were in our sleeping bags looking at the stars. He pulled out four very sexy panties that he had bought at my favorite store. He whispered, "Try them on in the moonlight." What a night!

But you may be getting in over your head. Certain pieces of lingerie may look good on one type of figure but not on another. Some bras and teddies, for example, are built for full-figured women, and others are built for small-busted women. Some are built for long-torsos and others for short. You can embarrass her royally if you present her with something that does not flatter her.

If you want to test the waters, point out a few sexy items in a catalog or advertisement and say, "Oh I'd like to see this on you!" and judge her reaction. You might even ask, "What would you do if I got you something like that?"

It may be that if she is comfortable with special lingerie, she'll want to buy it herself. You might offer to escort her to a lingerie department so that she can choose a few naughty pieces to delight you in back home.

Clothing Comes in Many Colors

Our survey respondents told us that they get more clothing than they want. We might accept that on face value, or we might analyze that response in light of this addendum:

> For every birthday, he buys me something new to wear, and I feel guilty because I never wear it. He just doesn't know my style, my size, or even the colors I look best in. Usually I sneak the item back, hoping he won't ask why I don't ever wear it.

Clothing *can* make a terrific gift, however, if you know your partner's sizes, favorite colors, needs, and likes and dislikes. If you have access to her closet, check out the labels of her favorite dresses. What are the brand names? What size? What color shoes does she have to match whatever you buy?

If you can, take a few of her favorite dresses to the department store where she buys clothes, and ask a sales person to find something in the same style. Ask a friend or relative she may shop with if something has caught her eye or if she has made any suggestions lately.

On the other hand, you might give her an afternoon of shopping—with you as her escort, of course.

Soufflé Pans Fall Flat

Household appliances? "I get too many of them." "They are definitely not romantic." "Why does he always see me as the cleaning lady?"

Things that relate to household chores were on the bottom of the list of romantic gifts.

But what if she really does want a blender? You *can* make something mundane a special and romantic gift by the way you give it. You can fill it with flowers, for example, or include a special small item in it that you know she will find romantic. (Just be sure she finds the hidden bracelet before she turns the blender on *puree.*)

Sports and Hobbies May Be Romantic

Most women do not consider receiving gifts related to their sports or hobbies as romantic, unless the gift is a large-ticket item that a woman feels is too expensive or extravagant for her to purchase on her own. An expensive bicycle for a bicyclist—especially if you ride with her—can be a great gift, for example. As one survey respondent told us:

> While we were remodeling our first house, I became interested in working with tile. I wanted a tile saw. But I knew that my husband would think it extravagant to spend money on such a thing, so I rented one—also at great expense—to refit the tile on the floor of the downstairs bathroom. There were still three bathroom floors and counters to go, as well as two fireplaces and a kitchen counter. And because of my interest, I was getting inquiries from friends about redoing their bathrooms and kitchens. When it came time for my birthday, we didn't have much, so Mark arranged a backyard barbecue with a group of our neighbors. It was a nice celebration, and I was pleased with the time and attention he spent in arranging it. But it wasn't until after the neighbors left that he gave me a package—a tile saw! I was shocked. It was the most romantic thing he had done yet.

Know your partner!

Activities to Hone Your Romantic Spirit

Following are examples of actions and activities which, according to our survey respondents, express the romantic spirit.

Try one or two now, and then come back later for more when
you feel comfortable enough to take a few more risks.

- Take her window-shopping—just for fun. Pass by a jewelry store, a clothing store, a travel agency. See what
  catches her eye. Make a mental note. In each situation,
  ask her questions about what she would want if she could
  choose. Tell her about what you want, just to keep her
  from suspecting anything. And by all means, do this far in
  advance of any gift-giving, lest she expect something she
  won't be getting. Just for fun.
- Go to Chapter 10, "Your Romance Notebook," and find
  out everything you can about what she wants in gifts from
  you.
- Plan a special occasion—her next birthday, your anniversary, whatever—and do it right. Make reservations at a romantic restaurant, send a love note invitation, make
  arrangements for child care, plant a special gift somewhere to surprise her (e.g., take it to the restaurant and
  instruct your waiter when to present it, or present it yourself over coffee or after-dinner drinks), investigate dance
  places you can suggest after dinner, and maybe even buy
  her something special to wear (or take her shopping for
  it).
- Give her a book of coupons to cash in at any time. Include household chores, breakfast in bed, cooking meals,
  shopping, walking her dog, gassing up her car, sexual
  favors—whatever you know she'd like.

Occasions Made Special

Our survey respondents had very definite opinions about
which occasions are important to celebrate. They rated "He remembers our anniversary or special day" highest, followed by
"He makes my birthday special." It's imperative that you find
out what occasions are most important to your own partner, of

course, but whatever her favorites are, our survey respondents can give you some advice on celebrating them.

For more help in planning your celebrations, see Chapter 8, "Great Dates."

Your Anniversary

You might expect that married women would place more importance on celebrating an anniversary than single women who have not been in a relationship very long, but that isn't the case. The majority of women—married and single—rate this day as tops—whether it is the anniversary of their first meeting, their first date, or their wedding. Celebrating that day is special to your partner because it reaffirms your relationship. It is a day that only the two of you share.

What is the best way to celebrate?

Your anniversary celebration should focus on the special relationship you have together. Here, the elements of romance—candlelight, moonlight, flowers, romantic sentiment, or reference to some romantic aspect of your early courtship—are particularly important.

Take time alone—this is definitely not the day to invite friends in for a barbecue—and use this day to celebrate your love for each other. So many of the women we heard from ranked "He arranges for us to have time alone" as very important to romance. If you have children, take a look at Chapter 6, "If She's a Mom," for some ideas on making time alone with your partner. For if there is one day in the year that you should spend alone with her, it's your anniversary.

If you don't already know what day she considers your anniversary—the day you met, your first date, the day you proposed, your wedding anniversary—find out now. Then, when the time comes to celebrate, take the initiative, and surprise her. If your anniversary falls on a day that would be difficult to celebrate this year, at least let her know that you are thinking of her—give her a love call, a love note, or a bouquet of her favorite flowers—and let her know what day you have planned to celebrate the special event.

A gift is nice but not necessary. If she follows tradition, you'll want to know what type of gift to give for each wedding anniversary:

Year 1: paper	Year 20: china
Year 5: wood	Year 25: silver
Year 10: tin	Year 50: gold
Year 15: crystal	Year 75: diamond

Whatever the gift, large or small, just be sure that it's romantic. Here's an example from one of our happier survey respondents:

> To celebrate our fiftieth wedding anniversary, my husband took me to a restaurant I had always wanted to try. It was glorious. He did everything right. We had a table overlooking the lake. Afterward, there was a dance band, and he requested "our" song—the one we danced to that first night. Then he ordered dessert. It was served with a heart-shaped crystal pendant set atop a scoop of coffee ice cream. He produced the gold chain from his pocket and fixed the clasp around my neck. In spite of all the ups and downs that have come since our first meeting, this was love all over again.

This was a fiftieth—very important—so don't let this most perfect situation intimidate you. But do note how special every detail was for the woman.

Most importantly, remember that this is a day to celebrate your love. Forget the unimportant things—if the food at the restaurant isn't up to par, the traffic is difficult, the parking expensive—make sure that nothing gets in the way of letting your partner know how special she is to you.

Her Birthday

Her birthday is another day that is unique for her. This is a day to demonstrate that you are glad she was born. Here, a special celebration as well as a special gift is in order. The gift may be something you know she has wanted, or it may be something that you know she'll just love. Or it may be a gift of time—either with you (a weekend pursuing one of her favorite interests), or "time off"—a gift for her to get away to a spa, a gift certificate for her to go shopping for herself while you mind the children, a massage by a professional, or a gift of housecleaning to lighten her load.

Most important, of course, is that you pay attention to her desires. Give her something that she wants. "I would like anything that reminded him of me," one woman wrote, "especially if he told me why."

For help in deciphering your own partner's desires, refer to Chapter 10, "Your Romance Notebook."

Valentine's Day

Valentine's Day, a commercial holiday celebrating romance, was ranked well below anniversaries and birthdays. Still, most women have the childhood wish to be their love's "Valentine."

Women really do like "mushy" cards, especially if you've composed the thought yourself. If you're in a new relationship, start with a card and maybe some flowers or a nice plant. Sexy lingerie is appropriate if you know what will flatter her figure. Adding a little perfumed sachet to the package is a definite plus.

Dinner out is nice, but you can also consider fixing dinner for her at home. Be sure to include the candlelight and something festive to drink. Let her know that you value your relationship with her.

By the way, though chocolates are promoted as a traditional Valentine's gift, and although sharing chocolates did enter into some of our survey respondents' romantic fantasies, *none* of our survey respondents indicated a desire to receive candy as a gift. But find out what your own partner desires.

Mother's Day

If your partner is the mother of your child or of children who live with you, you would be wise to celebrate Mother's Day.

A nice gift on Mother's Day is to spend time as a family. Wake her with a love note and a flower. Serve her breakfast in bed and plan a relaxing outing for the family. Or make a terrific family dinner. If the children are old enough, let them help out in celebrating their mother's special day. If the children are small and need special care, make a point of caring for their needs so that your partner can relax.

Besides receiving a token of *your* appreciation, your partner will also enjoy receiving something from her children. If the children are too young to shop, you can step in and try a little forgery.

Christmas and Hanukkah

Christmas and Hanukkah ranked at the bottom of the special days for romance, perhaps because of their religious significance or because they (especially Christmas) are thought of as mainly for children. For many women, this is a very hectic and tiring time.

These holidays do have a number of traditions associated with them, and the women who get special joy out of performing such traditions are particularly pleased when their partners willingly participate. One woman, for example, offered the following:

> The only romance in the holidays comes when my husband shares in the festivities. We walk out in the snow together to cut down the tree. At home we drag the lights and the ornaments out of the basement and spend an evening trimming the tree. My husband helps me choose some of the gifts and sometimes he even helps wrap the presents. There's usually a fire in the fireplace and hot cider on the stove. Sometimes we join the neighbors in caroling. We don't have any children yet ourselves, but one year he rented a costume and played Santa for the neighborhood kids. It was so much fun for both of us.

You might volunteer to escort her as she shops for children, friends, or parents. Invite her to take a break in the shopping day for lunch or a cappuccino at a restaurant in the mall. And while you're shopping with her, see if anything catches her eye—for her. Take note, and come back later and have it gift wrapped to surprise her on the special day.

The gifts that a woman might enjoy for Christmas or Hanukkah range across a wide spectrum. But if she must open her gift in front of others, try not to embarrass her with sexy things. Women love surprises, but this is one time when you could ask her to make a list of "wish" items, of which you might choose one. Then, in addition to the one you choose from her list, add another not on her list but that you know she would like—something romantic, of course.

Activities to Hone Your Romantic Spirit

- Discover which occasions are most special to her. If she doesn't mention your anniversary, celebrate it anyway. Try to find out what her expectations are for this event. Is this a big one—the first anniversary, the twenty-fifth, etc.? What would make her feel special—a special place, a special song, to be alone, to have a huge bash with all her friends? Find out far in advance, and then make it happen.
- Create or purchase a personal gift (something sensual— sight, touch, smell, feel) for no special reason. Find a special time when the two of you are alone and she is relaxed. Present it to her in a nicely wrapped package.
- Mail her a love note.
- Make note of any hints she drops about special occasions she would like to celebrate or gifts she would like to receive.

8

Great Dates

A Great Date is a special time that you share only with the woman you love. It's time set apart, where you can focus totally on one another. Although a Great Date is a great way to celebrate a birthday, anniversary, or other special day, you don't need to have a reason to plan for one. In fact, some of the greatest dates are the ones that come for no special reason. These can create some of the most treasured memories, like the following from one of our respondents:

> On Thursday night, he asked me to pack a bag for the weekend. "Casual clothes, walking shoes, something warm for a possible storm," he told me. He picked me up after work on Friday and we drove up through the woods to a little bed and breakfast on the lake. A bottle of cold champagne was waiting for us in the room. The quaint restaurant downstairs served a romantic candlelit dinner. The next day we walked along the shore. And when it got dark, we took a brisk naked swim. That weekend brought romance back into our relationship.

In our survey, we asked women to describe their romantic fantasies. You may be pleased to learn that not one fantasy mentioned being decked in diamonds, swathed in mink, or stolen away on a private yacht to Fantasy Island. No, the fantasies women of all ages across the country described were very attainable by the everyday, nine-to-five guy. To underline that fact, we present a representative sampling throughout this chapter.

Many of our survey respondents mentioned that men just don't understand how important romance is to a relationship. A Great Date is a wonderful way to demonstrate that at least *you* understand.

Planning for Romance

You'll need to do some up-front planning so that, when the time comes, you can both relax and have a good time. In this chapter, in fact, we ask you to do a lot of planning. And if you haven't yourself planned outings in the past, you might want to take it slowly. Don't let the checklists presented here send you running. In the beginning, at least, you may want to let your partner help out. But eventually, if you want to romance your lady with truly great dates, you'll need to take over.

Whether you're planning a picnic in the woods, a night on the town, or a week in the mountains, here are a few prerequisites to make sure that you're all set when she is.

Find Out What She Wants to Do

How does she enjoy spending her time? Whether you're planning for a simple evening out or an extended holiday, find out her preferences.

Most of the women who answered our survey told us that they love surprises. If your Great Date is to be a surprise, discover her desires far in advance of the event so she doesn't suspect. (Refer to Chapter 10, "Your Romance Notebook.")

Determine in general where she would like to go and what she would like to do. What has she had the most fun doing in the past? What has she asked to do? What does she wish for?

For an evening date, does she have a favorite restaurant, or is there one she has wanted to try? Does she enjoy the symphony, the ballet, the opera, or the theater?

Does she like to participate in outdoor sporting activities, such as hiking, boating, skiing, or biking? Or would she rather kick back and relax, perhaps soaking up the sun, or soaking in a hot tub? How about sight-seeing, antiquing, or visiting an amusement park? Do we dare mention shopping . . . ?

For an overnight trip, would she rather stay at a hotel in the city or a secluded cottage on a lake or in the mountains? Or would she prefer a resort or spa? Maybe she'd like to get away from the cold in the winter, from the heat in summer, or maybe tour the foliage in the fall?

Perhaps she would enjoy returning to the spot of your first truly romantic date—where you met, or where you proposed to her?

Here's what one of our respondents wrote:

> When he suggested that we go on a rafting trip, I was amazed that he remembered. It had been months since I mentioned I wanted to try it. In the meantime, unbeknownst to me, he had gotten information on different rivers and rafting trips and found an organization that was perfect for our skill level. I didn't know he was such a good planner. Or such a romantic!

The important thing is to make sure you're doing something that *she* enjoys. If you truly don't know how she would like to spend her special time, ask her.

For many women, the planning can be almost as fun as the event itself. Does your special woman enjoy participating in the plans, or would she prefer that you do all the up-front planning and then surprise her?

Check Out the Options

The setting for a Great Date is important. Make sure it's romantic. And make sure that the two of you will be able to spend time alone. (This is not the time to share with friends.) Check out the various options that would satisfy her.

If you're ordering tickets to a music or theater performance, ask about the best available seating.

If you want to find a good restaurant, watch your local newspaper for reviews. Ask friends who appreciate the same kind of food that your partner does.

If you're looking for a certain kind of lodging, check the back sections of relevant magazines. Watch the Sunday travel section in the paper. Call a travel agent. Check local resources. If possible, make an on-site inspection. Ask questions about privacy, food, availability of romantic rooms with views, fireplaces, Jacuzzis. If it's too far to visit, ask friends or other acquaintances who may be familiar with the place. Call and ask to have brochures or photos sent.

Determine Your Budget

There may be inexpensive ways to satisfy expensive tastes. If you live in a college or university town, you have rich opportunities to enjoy music, theater, and intellectual events. These things usually aren't well publicized, so call the school to find out what's happening. Many communities have civic events— plays, concerts, lectures—that are very reasonably priced. So when you can't swing the cost of symphony tickets or the trip to Broadway, try a local performance or a concert in the park.

Don't put off romantic time together while you're saving for the BIG event, either. Do what you can along the way. If you can't afford a week in the Alps, a nearby ski lodge may be just fine. Even a picnic in the woods can be romantic if you've done some up-front planning.

Check Her Schedule

Determine whether the Great Date can be a surprise. If it is not planned to be a surprise, you can simply ask her about her schedule. But if you do want to surprise her, you'll have to do some sleuthing to find out when she's available. This may also involve finding out when others are free. (You wouldn't want to plan a great romantic evening alone on the night that Little Jimmy debuts in the school play.)

Actualize Your Plan

Women have told us that they end up making all the arrangements. For your Great Date, handle as much of it yourself as you think your partner would like—even if you do need to ask her for the phone number of Little Mary's favorite baby-sitter.

Here are some of the things you may need to do:

- Make reservations or order tickets. For a choice of good seats (at the play or on a plane), you may need to do this months in advance.
- Arrange for child care, pet care, plant care. Alert neighbors if you plan to be away for more than a day. If you would like it to be a surprise, let others who rely on your partner know that she won't be available for the duration, or let them know where they can reach you.
- If this Great Date is a dinner at home, arrange for the food. Buy the groceries or call the caterer. Arrive home before she does, and set the mood: low lighting (candles?), romantic music, flowers on the table. Turn off the TV and the telephone (unless you have children off at a baby-sitter's; then *you* answer the phone or the door, and let anyone else know to call back the next day).
- If your partner will need to take time from her job to go away with you, make sure you give her enough notice.
- Make travel arrangements. If you're driving, make sure the car is clean, gassed up, and operating well. If you're flying or going by public transportation, collect the tickets, maps, itinerary, rental car and room confirmations, and emergency phone numbers so that you'll be ready to go.
- At some point, you will have to tell her about the plan. If you're taking her to a special setting for only an evening

or an afternoon, you can get by with merely suggesting what she might wear—hiking boots or an evening dress. If she needs special clothes for the event, you might even surprise her with a package when you tell her of the event, or plan to take her shopping while you're away. But if the trip involves a week's worth of clothing, shoes, jewelry, and toiletries, you'd better give her enough time to do her own packing (and to do needed laundry and shopping, as well). But even then, the telling will be a great surprise for her.

- Obtain any equipment needed for planned activities, or arrange for equipment rental or purchase on your arrival. Do you need a picnic basket, tennis rackets, or maybe mountain bikes? Make sure ahead of time that you will have these things when they're needed, lest you waste precious moments when you reach your destination.
- Pick her up and go.

As mentioned earlier, women told us that they're usually left to handle the details—things that their partners wouldn't even know to do. But we were pleased to find that at least a few men out there paid attention. Here's what one of our respondents offered:

> He had arranged for everything. I kept asking about all the little things I worry about whenever we have to go somewhere—putting out the cat food, setting the light timer, giving the key to the neighbor, getting the traveler's checks, stopping the mail and newspaper, watering the plants—and he had thought of it all. This was truly amazing.

Before finalizing any plans, be sure to find out what all the details are.

And if you want the Great Date to be really special, pay special attention to your partner in the days preceding the date. Try to avoid her "hot buttons." Any insensitivity on your part could totally destroy the mood you've tried so hard to attain.

Activities to Hone Your Romantic Spirit

Following are examples of actions and activities which, according to our survey respondents, express the romantic spirit. Try one or two now, and then come back later for more when you feel comfortable enough to take a few more risks.

- Begin to take note of what she asks to do or when she says, "If only we could. . . ." You might want to suggest to her some of the things you believe she would enjoy, not letting on that you are making any plans: "Bill and Mary went ballooning last week. They said it was great fun." See how she responds. Or, "Have you ever thought about maybe going for a two-day bike tour? Do you think that would be fun?"
- Start planning for some options. Once you have some "leads" from her, check the newspapers, the Yellow Pages, or call a travel agency. Ask some of your friends about where to get more information about certain places or activities. Or plan together with your partner.
- Determine how much you can spend on this Great Date. If you share expenses with your partner, make sure you're not going to shock her with something extravagant of which she would not approve.
- Check your schedules and begin to actualize your plan.
- Go back to some of the exercises in previous chapters that help make her feel desirable, special, your Number One priority. And help her feel truly special.

The Romantic Dinner

In defining romantic activities, nearly all our survey respondents put "romantic dinners"—in home or out—high on the list. Usually the woman does the cooking in the household, so for her, having someone else prepare a special dinner is like taking a vacation.

But what constitutes a romantic dinner?

Seek an Intimate Mood

A romantic dinner requires an intimate mood, which can be created in a restaurant, in a meadow, on a mountain top, or even at home. The two prerequisites for a romantic mood are (1) that you are together, away from all distractions (including people you know), and (2) that you focus on each other for an extended and unrushed period of time.

Choose a romantic setting.

If it's a do-it-yourself date and you're not comfortable with your own cooking skills, you should be able to find a catering service that will set up a romantic dinner at home. In fact, you can create a romantic dinner anywhere. Rent a rowboat and take a picnic to the park across the lake. Even a picnic in the backyard can be romantic, if the setting is quiet and secluded. How about a tablecloth in front of the fireplace or on the back porch? No reservations needed. (If there are children at home, refer to Chapter 6, "If She's a Mom," for ideas on getting time alone with her.) And don't leave things for her to clean up.

If you're seeking a restaurant, does she have a favorite place already? When were you there last? Would she rather return to a special spot or go somewhere new? If you need ideas, get recommendations from friends, newspaper reviews, and magazines that review restaurants in your area.

A romantic setting includes atmosphere. Go and check it out, or ask someone you trust (someone other than the folks who work there). A restaurant set in a romantic spot can be special, but what's *inside* the door matters most. Check the lighting, the music, and the noise level.

A restaurant broken into small, intimate rooms is much more romantic than a big barnlike place. Tables should be spaced well apart for intimate conversation. And the restaurant should be warm enough for your partner to be comfortable.

Low light, particularly candlelight, is best for romance.

Restaurants conducive to romance will use cloth napkins and, most likely, cloth tablecloths as well.

Service is important. You'll want a restaurant where your server is alert to your needs—always there when needed, but not bothering you otherwise. He or she should never intrude upon your intimacy. As you finish each course, dishes should be taken discreetly and quietly away. You don't want to hear things clashing or be left with dirty silverware for the next course.

A romantic restaurant will appreciate that you two want to spend time together, lingering over your meal. Make sure you choose a place where you won't be told that others are waiting for your table.

Soft, slow music helps set the mood—as long as it's the music that she likes. Instrumental is generally more romantic than vocals, because it doesn't interfere with conversation. Live music is a plus—a piano, a guitar, or a small chamber orchestra, for example. Another romantic plus is a dance floor; if she likes to dance, step to it. Slow cheek-to-cheek dancing is the closest thing to sex in public. If you don't know how, you might want to take a few lessons in advance.

And let's not forget about the quality of the food. Something a little different from the ordinary is nice. Most medium-sized towns have a variety of international restaurants from which to choose. Check restaurant reviews in your local paper, ask friends whom you trust to have good taste, or go there yourself and try it. But make sure she will also enjoy that type of food. If you're not sure, ask her. If you want to romance her, take the time and the initiative to find a special place that she will like.

Here are some tips from one of our survey respondents:

I guess I'm pretty lucky because my husband is a retired chef. Not only do we have great romantic dinners at home, but he loves to go out and try good restaurants himself. He routinely reads restaurant reviews. And wherever we go, he's always on the lookout for good places. Whether or not we plan to eat out that night, he will walk into restaurants in the middle of the day to look at the menu and ask how things are prepared. If it's not busy, he'll even ask if he can have a look in the kitchen. It pays off in the end, for we have great meals. Also, the maitre d' usually recognizes him from the earlier meeting, so we're always seated in the best areas.

Make the Reservation

Make the reservation well in advance so *you* can choose the day and *you* can choose the time.

Are there certain areas in the restaurant that are more conducive to romance than others? If so, when making a reservation, request the table in that cozy little spot, or the one by the window with the view of the lake or the city lights. By all means, make sure that you will be seated *well away* from swinging kitchen doors and noisy bussing stations.

If you're celebrating a special occasion, ask what the restaurant can do for you. Balloons on her chair with the wait staff singing "Happy Birthday" might be fun, but it is *not* very romantic. How about a special dessert with a single tall candle? Or maybe the chef could write "Happy Anniversary Susie" in chocolate around the plate.

Go in Style

Give your partner plenty of warning about dress so she won't be embarrassed by being either overdressed or underdressed for the evening. You don't need to tell her where you are taking her, but you might suggest something from her closet. (Women are especially pleased when a partner asks her to wear the "blue dress that matches your eyes," that "red dress that makes men turn their heads," or "the pearl earrings I gave you." That's a clear sign that you're paying attention.)

You might suggest that she get a new dress. Better yet, take her shopping and help her pick it out. Or you might want to pick out something for her yourself and present it to her the evening you're going out. Do this only if you're sure of her size, the colors she enjoys wearing, and her favorite style. One of our respondents told us her romantic fantasy:

> He sneaks one of my favorite dresses out of my closet and takes it to the department store where I usually buy my clothes. He tells the salesperson the name of the restaurant (she of course is familiar with it) and he asks her for a dress similar to my favorite one for a special evening at that restaurant. Another salesperson my size tries on a series of dresses, from which my partner chooses one that he knows will look terrific on me. He even remembers the colors of my shoes to coordinate with the new dress. He calls me at work one Friday afternoon and tells me to be ready for something special. When I arrive home, he's waiting. He presents the box to me. I open the box. The dress is perfect. I put it on. I look gorgeous. He escorts me to the car and whisks me off to a hideaway restaurant with a romantic setting for the most luscious evening together. We dine. We dance. He tells me wonderful things. We can't keep our hands off each other in the car on the way home. Back home, we fall into each other's arms and fill the night with cries of love.

On the other hand, she may want to choose the restaurant and decide for herself what to wear. Know what she wants.

Great dates demand lots of planning. That includes great grooming. In order to escort your lady on this Great Date, be sure to shower, shave (even if you've already shaved that morning), and put on her favorite cologne or after-shave. Clean your fingernails. Make sure your clothes are clean and ironed (don't wait until it's time to leave to find out that your best shirt is in the laundry). Shine your shoes. Wear a good suit or sports jacket and coordinated slacks. Make sure you have a silk tie that works well with your outfit. And if you're the continental type, put a silk handkerchief into your breast pocket—one that picks up the colors of your tie. Ok! Now you look terrific. You feel terrific. After all, this is a Great Date.

For an added touch, when you come home or arrive to pick her up, hand her a bouquet of flowers. Or just a single rose in one of her favorite colors.

Plan for a Leisurely Evening

Do not schedule anything after dinner. A romantic dinner is romantic in itself. Rushing off to a play, movie, or game could take the romance out of the evening.

But that doesn't mean you must go right home, either. Actually, it's good to prolong the romance of the evening by taking your partner off to another romantic spot. Appropriate activities to follow a romantic dinner are those that do not require a timed arrival: walk to the rooftop bar for a nightcap, drop in on a romantic dancing spot, drive to the shore or a high point overlooking the city for a bit of necking. But whatever it is, don't rush. And don't worry if you don't make it there. Romance is living in the present.

Let's repeat that. Romance is living in the present. There is no past and no future. Only you and that woman you love, right here, right now. Ok, so maybe you're not a Buddhist monk, but paying attention to the present will help you develop your romantic attitude.

And what do you talk about when you're being leisurely? Dinner conversation can make or break a romantic evening. The successful romantic will focus on his partner. And just to make sure, come armed with two items of conversation that would interest *her.*

A few dos and don'ts gathered from our survey respondents:

She Wants to Hear About	She Doesn't Want to Hear About
• How wonderful she looks	• The kids, the in-laws
• How you miss her	• The office
• How good it is to be with her	• Looking forward to something that doesn't involve her
• Plans for your future together	
• What you like about your relationship	• Anything negative, anything you don't like about *anything*
• Plans for her future (to meet her personal dreams, goals, etc.)	• Topics that you disagree on that may cause an argument
• Her interests (encourage her in them)	• Chores

(continues)

- How you met (reminisce about the wonderful beginnings)
- Why she's special to you
- Positive things about the restaurant
- Her accomplishments
- Her day
- Her ideas
- The appreciation you have for all she does

- Expenses, bills, taxes
- Problems of today
- Other women, past or present
- Negative things about the restaurant
- Your accomplishments
- Your day
- Your ideas
- The difficulties you had in planning this Great Date

If your partner should bring up a topic that you feel might spoil the romance, just listen, and then try to gently steer away from it with an open-ended question about her: "Have you ever considered what you might want to be doing in ten years?"

And what do you do while she's talking? Respond. Focus on her eyes. Nod in agreement. Show interest when she shares new thoughts or ideas with you. Use phrases such as "I know what you mean," "Really?" "I didn't know you felt that way," "Tell me more." Do not try to compete with her in "conversation time." Just listen.

Of course it goes without saying that if you invite her on a Great Date, you pay. Do not even consider an offer for her to share. Pick up the bill as soon as it's placed on the table and put it where she cannot get to it. Don't look at it for a while (and don't let her see it at all). Just relax. It's not a concern. This is romance. If she insists on paying half, tell her she can romance *you* one day. If you're upset or shocked at the price, don't let her know that, either. Instead, quietly call any problems to the attention of the server. You're in charge here, and you only want to please her.

Activities to Hone Your Romantic Spirit

- Check out romantic dining spots in your area. Take a little time to go to each of them, look at the menu, ask about dinner lighting and music (it would be best if you went while they were serving dinner), take a peek at the plates coming from the kitchen, notice the room arrangement, and determine which table you would like to reserve. Ask about special arrangements that could be made for a special occasion.

- Check out what to do after a romantic dinner. Is there a scenic spot or drive in your area? A place to do some slow dancing? Or a quiet little spot where you can have a night-cap?

- Invite her to a night of romance at home. Send the children off to the neighbors or with their favorite sitter for the night. Show up in your most enticing clothes—whether it's jeans and flannels or a tux. Have a bottle of champagne chilling in the refrigerator. Hand her a bouquet of flowers. Arrange dinner ahead of time (i.e., bring home her favorite carry-outs, order from a caterer, trade a romance meal night with a neighbor, cook up something sensual . . . get creative). Put on romantic music. Light a candle—or a fire. Rev up that romantic spirit to let her know in so many ways how wonderful she is.

The Romantic Getaway

There is nothing like a change of scenery to get a couple out of a routine and into romance. Like the romantic dinner, a romantic getaway can be accomplished in a variety of ways—some costly, some not.

If you're planning a trip of a few days or more, you may want to involve your partner early in the discussions so you don't spend money on something that she doesn't want to do or is unable to do. Also, many women have fun planning for a special trip. Just the fact that you initiate it is romantic. But of course, if you can tell her that you will take care of all the arrangements, that's a real romantic plus.

The most important aspect of the trip is that *you* take the initiative to plan some special time away for just the two of you.

Seek Romantic Places to Stay

If you live in the country, a few days in the city might be exciting. But if you live in a city, you may want to head for the hills. The important thing to keep in mind is what *she* likes to do. Here are some possibilities:

- Biking, reading, lounging at a country inn or bed and breakfast
- Enjoying the surf at a hotel by the seashore
- Swimming, boating, or just relaxing at a cottage by the lake
- Exploring good food, shops, and culture in the city
- Improving your game at a golf or tennis resort
- Camping or backpacking in the woods
- Touring a national park
- Driving across country in a car or rented camper
- Flying to another continent and exploring the sights
- Flying to a sunny island
- Scuba diving or snorkeling
- Cruising to Alaska, the Caribbean, or the Mediterranean
- Volunteering with a local, national, or international environmental or human welfare organization
- Working on a dude ranch
- Working out at a health spa
- Visiting a commercial theme park
- Antiquing in small country towns
- Attending a world's fair
- Attending the Olympics
- Driving or biking through New England or the Great Lakes in the fall
- Skiing in the Sierras, the Rockies, or the Alps
- Wine tasting in upstate New York, California, Oregon, Washington, or Texas
- Mountain climbing
- White-water rafting or kayaking down a river

Many books available in libraries and bookstores provide details on the locations, amenities, and prices of these and other getaways. Friends and coworkers may also have suggestions. Major newspapers (the Sunday travel section, for example) carry ads and write-ups on numerous places to visit. And of course, you can always check with a travel agent, where you can find free maps, brochures, and advice.

It's important to start planning well in advance in order to have the widest accommodation choices and the best travel fares, particularly if you plan to go to a place during its "high" season.

On the other hand, you may want to keep your eyes open for off-season promotional rates. The ski resort during the rainy season or the beach in winter can make for greater intimacy, especially if the tourists have all gone home. And this kind of trip can be arranged more easily on the spur of the moment.

When you finally do make the reservations, ask about local highlights, activities, and restaurants. And when you arrive at your destination, ask your host for recommendations on things to do.

One of our survey respondents shared a romantic weekend away:

I'm a landscape designer, divorced, with children. I rarely get away from my own area, just north of Chicago. But one of my clients has a property in Wisconsin on Lake Michigan and asked that I go up there and provide a design. My boyfriend asked if he could go along. He told me he'd drive, he'd make all the arrangements for a weekend away, and he'd find a nice place for dinner, so I should bring a good dress. He enlisted the help of his sister to take my children for the weekend. Then, on the sly, he called my client and asked for a recommendation for a romantic place to stay and to have dinner. We stayed at a terrific bed and breakfast right on the lake and had a marvelous time together. I had never had such a special time with anyone. I think I'll take him along more often!

Take Care of Arrangements

Be sure to take into account what your partner will need to feel comfortable. If you're comfortable sleeping in the great outdoors with nothing between you and the stars, it doesn't mean your partner wouldn't appreciate a tent. Don't expect her to pack the car with you or provide the food, either. This is your turn to take care of the details and do the work. One of our respondents wrote:

> After Greg and I were married a few years, we were having some problems with our relationship. Greg suggested that we get away somewhere and focus on each other. We planned the whole thing together, but for the first time he offered to do a lot of the up-front work. We didn't have a lot of money at the time, so we didn't go far, but afterward we both agreed that that one weekend away saved our relationship—and brought the romance back into our lives.

If children are a part of the relationship, it is important that you consider how they will be cared for—even if they are hers, not yours. (See Chapter 6, "If She's a Mom.")

If you put enough planning into the time away, you're sure to have a Great Date.

Activities to Hone Your Romantic Spirit

- Ask your partner how she would like to spend her time if she could get away for a weekend or maybe for a week or longer. Ask her what type of locations interest her—the city, the mountains, the ocean. From what she tells you, try to determine the options you have to please her, within your budget.
- Compare schedules and begin to narrow your options. Check out bookstores, the library, and travel agencies to discover the perfect Great Date.

- Follow through, yourself, on all arrangements. Ask your partner for pointers on certain aspects of the planning as you go along, just to make sure you meet her expectations about what needs to be done.
- Have fun!

9

One-Minute Romancer

Today we live in a fast-food, 24-hour teller, instant-gratification society. Nobody wants to wait in line. Nobody wants to wait for anything. (Will you please get to the point. . . !)

Ok. So here are 60 one-minute ways to romance your wonderful lady. Well, some might take more than just a minute. But in spite of the short time it takes to implement any one of these ideas, each carries a big impact—every one creates an opportunity to make a lasting impression. Just pick a number and go for it.

Each time you take advantage of one of these romantic ideas (or one of your own), you not only impress your partner, but you also grow your romantic spirit.

Now, just so you won't read the list with the best of intentions and then put this book at the bottom of your nightstand drawer for "future reference," get out your calendar and choose something for at least one day each week. One week you might choose Wednesday—send flowers. The next week Monday—request her favorite song. Come Friday two weeks from now, bring home a romantic video tape. On Saturday, use your own idea (after all, you know her better than we do). Get the picture?

1. Greet her when she arrives at the door. Go to her, hug her, and give her a kiss.
2. Pay her a compliment about her appearance. Be specific.

3. Order a "vanity" license plate for *your* car with *her* nickname—or better yet, something like "ILUVLUC."

4. Call her during the day and invite her on a date tonight: you'll pick her up and take her to a special restaurant, and afterward, maybe dancing . . . ?

5. Write her a love note and either send it in the mail or hide it where she's sure to find it.

6. Stop at a lingerie store or department store and pick up something seductive for her to wear tonight.

7. Bring her morning coffee, tea, or juice to her.

8. Put on her favorite music before she arrives home.

9. Invite her to go along on an upcoming business trip.

10. Bathe her. Wash her hair.

11. Buy a book you can read to each other in bed tonight—either romantic poetry or erotic stories, whichever *she* would like best.

12. Pick up a bouquet of fresh-cut flowers on the way to see her tonight and hand them to her with a kiss when you arrive.

13. Check your local paper, city magazine, or phone book to find a local spot you've never been to before (a small museum, a wildlife preserve, a park . . .) and invite her to explore it with you.

14. Give her a terrific massage (ok, so let's make this more than 60 seconds).

15. Show up at her place of work just before noon and invite her out to lunch (if she has other plans, don't pout—make a date for another day).

16. Ask her what she would like to do or see one day—something special—and then arrange for it to happen.

17. Help her put on a piece of jewelry.

18. Call her in the middle of the day just to tell her you're thinking of her. If you get her voice mail, leave a loving message.

19. Light a fire for her.

20. On a cold wintry morning, de-ice her car for her: scrape the windows, warm up the inside, and if necessary, shovel the walk to the car and the driveway behind it.
21. Carry in the groceries for her.
22. Pick up a romantic video that she's been wanting to see—and maybe dinner?
23. Make plans to revisit the place where you first met — the park around the corner or on the other side of the world—and celebrate.
24. Put candles on the table at dinner time.
25. Ask for her grocery list and do the shopping.
26. Take her outside to gaze at the moon and snuggle.
27. Pull out her chair for her when she's about to sit down at the dinner table. Put her napkin on her lap. Serve her.
28. Tell her how wonderful her hair smells.
29. Sing to her.
30. Invite her to a barbecue in the backyard (offer to do the planning, shopping, cooking, and cleanup).
31. Invite her to join you in a sporting activity or cultural event in which neither of you has participated before (maybe roller-blading, attending an opera, or renting mountain bikes).
32. Give her an evening off—to read, bathe, watch TV, shop, jog, or whatever—and take care of everything for her.
33. Order tickets to a special performance that she will enjoy.
34. While she eats, feed her from your plate as well as from her own (little morsels just every once in a while, between her own bites).
35. Give her a book of coupons for specific chores that you are willing to do for her whenever she wants to cash them in ("Good for one trip to the grocery" "... car wash,"

" . . .kitchen cleanup," " . . .vacuuming," " . . .baby diapering," " . . .dinner out," " . . .baby-sitting").

36. Surprise her with an unexpected hug and kiss.
37. Take her for a walk in the rain or snow.
38. Flirt. Give her the eye. Tease her. Touch her. Play. Have fun.
39. Leave a little surprise for her to find in her lingerie drawer or her cosmetic bag or her refrigerator after you've left for the day or before you arrive home— something that would make her smile (a music CD or tape, a book by her favorite author, a small bottle of her favorite perfume, a silk rose or a real rose . . .).
40. Give her a loving nickname that tells her something special about her. Use it.
41. When you're with a group, compliment her. Touch her hand, kiss her gently on the neck, pay attention to her.
42. Take her shopping for something she needs or wants (and stay with her until she finds it).
43. Give her a gift certificate for time at a local spa: massage, facial, mud wrap.
44. Pick up fixings for a terrific dinner that you can prepare together.
45. Turn on the music and ask her to dance.
46. Take her to the highest point in your locality (a hike to the top of a hill or an elevator to the top of the tallest building) and look down on the scene below.
47. Pack a picnic and take her to the park or the beach.
48. Serve her breakfast in bed—with a flower.
49. Make reservations for a date at the place where you had your first real date, even if it involves flying half-way across the continent.
50. Remember that dress, bracelet, or purse she admired in the store window? Go get it for her.
51. Call your local florist and order her favorite flowers, to be delivered to wherever she is.

52. Think of one thing that you appreciate about her—and tell her. Just one thing. Make it specific: the way she looks, the way she acts, something she has done for you, a professional or intellectual accomplishment—whatever you appreciate right now.
53. In the morning, make the bed.
54. Call in a song request to her favorite radio station to be played when you know she'll be listening. Tell the announcer to be sure to say it's from you to your lovely lady (use her name or love nickname).
55. Make a trip to your local stationery store and buy some special stationery and matching envelopes. Send her a love letter.
56. Ask her what she would wish for, given a falling star. Over the following weeks, months, or years, remember that wish and do all you can to help her make it come true.
57. Ask her advice on something you feel is important.
58. Undress her slowly, touching her, noticing every wonderful thing about her body.
59. Warm up her side of the bed for her before she gets in.
60. Say "I love you."

Sweet dreams!

10

Your Romance Notebook

If you've read the previous chapters, you have a pretty good idea of what most women want in romance. But you also know that every woman is an individual. One woman may *expect* a man to open doors for her, another may find it *romantic*, and yet a third may see it as a *threat* to her independence. One woman may delight in receiving sexy lingerie, whereas another may be unwilling to wear it because it does not flatter her. One woman may love to receive a surprise ticket to a romantic weekend getaway, but another would rather be involved in the planning of it.

What does your own partner desire?

Answering the questions that follow will help you know your partner better—and help you move toward the romantic attitude that will please her. Be prepared for some surprises. But know that even small changes can make big differences in your romance.

For some of the questions, asking your partner outright may be appropriate (e.g., "What is the baby-sitter's phone number?"). But for most of the questions, you should be able to find out the answers just by listening to what she says on a day-to-day basis—and then checking out her verbal and nonverbal reactions to anything you try. Just remember that the element of surprise itself is romantic. Even in your questioning, don't give away too much. Play the private investigator.

As you discover each answer to what pleases your partner, think about how that bit of information will help you better romance her.

You may want to purchase a small notebook in which to record your findings. You might divide it into two sections: (1) what your partner desires, and (2) ways you can fulfill her desires. (For ideas on fulfilling her desires, you may want to revisit the exercises in earlier chapters of this book.)

While you're carrying out your investigation, however, it's important to keep in mind that you do *not* have to act on every suggestion. Some of her desires may be unreasonable, impractical, or simply distasteful for you to satisfy. The main objective here is to become more aware of what *pleases* your partner. Acting on even some of the smallest bits of information on a regular basis will help you develop your romantic attitude—and bring a higher level of romance to your relationship.

What Romance Means for Her

- What special times have you and your partner spent together that she has particularly enjoyed or remembered?
- What special things have you done for her that particularly pleased her?
- If she could have a wish come true, what would she wish for?
- What makes her feel special?
- Does your partner feel that she is your first priority? If not, what can you do to help her know that she is?
- What do you do that makes her laugh or smile?
- Does she think you are fun to be with? Do you flirt with her? What is her response?
- When you first met, where did you go and what did you do? What was it that excited her about you? What did she look forward to in a relationship with you?
- Does she feel that you would stand by her in anything? If not, what can you do to instill that feeling in her?

- What are her capabilities? Does she feel that you appreciate her capabilities? What can you do to bolster her self-esteem?
- Does she ask for compliments or for you to notice her? What in particular has she called to your attention?
- What are some of the particulars about her that you appreciate—the major things as well as the minor? Include the things you enjoy most about the way she looks, the way she acts, what she does professionally, what she does for you, what she does for others (including children), special aspects of her personality, and what turns you on about this woman.
- Do you give her compliments about those things that you most appreciate? How does she respond?
- Does she ever question your love for her? What specifically makes her anxious about your love for her? How can you help her know that you truly love her?
- Does she appreciate traditional manners (e.g., having a man open a door for her)?
- Does she feel that you respect every aspect of her life? If not, which aspects could you be more attentive to or supportive of?
- What has your partner seen other couples do that she found particularly romantic?
- Ask her to name the films she finds most romantic. What about them specifically is romantic?
- Does she have a favorite romantic hero? Why does she find him romantic?
- Has she ever asked you to do something romantic for her? What was it?
- Has she ever complained about your lack of romance in the way that you treat her? What specifically does she not want you to do? What would she rather you do?
- What personal habits of yours annoy her?
- What are some of your personal qualities that she finds most appealing?

How You Communicate

- Does she feel that you share enough information with her about how you spend your day, about your ideas, desires, goals, or plans?
- Has she ever complained that you weren't listening to her when she was telling you something? Are there particular topics which she feels you avoid?
- What are the best times to call her during the day or evening just to say hello?
- What topics of conversation does she most enjoy?
- What topics cause disagreements? Will simply listening to her concerns and problems end the argument? Or is there an action you can take to resolve the differences?
- When she tells you her problems, does she want help in solving them or just a supportive ear?
- Would she prefer that you share more of your problems with her?
- Is there anything that you do (or don't do) that makes her particularly angry or upset?
- Have you given her a "love nickname" that she enjoys?
- Has she ever written you love letters or love notes? What message did they convey?
- Have you ever written love notes or letters to her? What was her reaction?

How You Spend Time Together

- Do you take time for romance every day?
- Does she feel that you spend enough "quality time" alone with her? What would she like to do during that time?
- What do you do on evenings when you are together? Is this something your partner enjoys? Would your partner rather do something else at times?
- Does your partner like to dance, or would she like to learn? Would she like you to learn how to dance better? Would she

like you to go dancing with her? Do you know where to go dancing in your area?

- Are there any household chores that really get her down? Is there a way you can help her alleviate the problem (e.g., hire outside help, buy her a new appliance), or should you offer to help her do the chores yourself?
- Does she feel part of your life? Would she like to be included in some of the activities that you engage in alone, or would she like you to share in some of her activities?
- What is her daily schedule? When can you slip in and leave a surprise for her to find?
- What new activities could you pursue together?
- Does she feel she is in good physical health? Does she need encouragement to pursue activities that would be beneficial to her health?
- Does she feel that you are in good physical health? If not, what would she change about your lifestyle to make you healthier?
- Does she have enough free time for herself? What could you do to help free up more time for her?
- Would she appreciate a surprise visit from you during the day to invite her out for lunch? Do you know her work schedule so that you can plan spontaneous events during the day?
- Are there places in your community that offer inexpensive entertainment that she would enjoy (e.g., college or university plays, community theater, concerts in the park)?
- What kind of films does she like to see? When you go to a movie theater (or video store) together, does she choose the film or do you?
- What is her favorite kind of food? What varieties of wine does she enjoy?
- What sort of food would she like you to cook? What are you capable of cooking? Is that an interest you could pursue together?

- Ask her to describe a romantic evening at home, and then a romantic evening out.
- Ask her to describe a romantic weekend together.
- Ask her to describe a romantic dream vacation.
- Does she feel that you take enough time to get away together (just the two of you) for mini-vacations (e.g., weekends away)?
- Do you take lengthier vacations together at places where you can get away alone for a while? What would she like to do on a vacation?
- Would she like to spend more time in nature, lolling at the beach, hiking in the woods, or driving to the mountains?
- What romantic dining spots (within your budget) are available in your area?
- What sort of restaurant does she most enjoy? What type of food? What is the atmosphere? Why does she enjoy that restaurant? What other restaurants can you check out to see if they're her style?
- Do you know the name and phone number of her supervisor at work? Would your partner feel comfortable if you called to ask for time off for your partner for a special surprise occasion?
- Does she enjoy breakfast in bed?
- What special date would she enjoy most: restaurant, theater, opera, ballet, museum, antiquing, dancing, shopping, participation or spectator sports, amusement park?
- Could you pack for your partner? Do you know where she keeps her cosmetics, her lingerie, what she needs for a weekend trip? Or would she rather pack for herself?
- Does she like surprise events? Or would she rather take part in the planning?

Choosing Gifts

- What occasions are most important to your partner—her birthday, your marriage anniversary, the anniversary of the

day you met, Mother's Day, Valentine's Day, Christmas, Hanukkah, other?
- What type of gifts has she asked for in the past?
- What gifts have you given her that she appreciated more than others, used often, or cherishes still?
- Is she involved in a sport or hobby that requires special equipment or clothing that you could purchase for her? Would she find a gift of that sort romantic?
- Would she find a gift related to her business or career romantic?
- Does she like to go window-shopping with you? What catches her eye when she walks by a clothing store, a jewelry store, or a travel agency?
- What kind of small surprises would she appreciate receiving for no special reason except to let her know that you are thinking of her? Do you have a personal calendar where you can pencil in at least one surprise per week (in code, if necessary)?
- Buying clothes:
  - What sort of clothing would she like to receive from you (e.g., business clothes, dressy clothes, lingerie)?
  - Would she prefer that you surprise her with them? Or would she rather you took her shopping for them?
  - What are her favorite colors (in order of preference)? What colors does she like to wear? What colors does she look best wearing? What colors are her shoes?
  - What are her clothing sizes (check her favorite things for sizes): dress, blouse, sweater, slacks, shoes, bra, panties, stockings?
  - Would she be comfortable wearing lingerie that you buy her, or would she rather choose those she feels are the most flattering on her?
- What style of jewelry does she enjoy wearing—for everyday, for evening? Has she ever admired jewelry in magazines, store windows, on other women—a gold bracelet, jewel earrings, or a watch perhaps?

- What is her favorite scent? Is it available in perfume, soap, lotion, bubble bath? Would she use such products?
- What kind of music does she enjoy? Does she use tapes, CDs, or records?
- What sorts of gifts does she most enjoy receiving for no special reason, and what sorts of gifts does she enjoy receiving for special occasions? Flowers? Jewelry? Clothing? Work-related items? Sports-related items? Perfumed toiletries? Tools or equipment for hobbies? Household items? Love notes from you? Other?

Bringing Romance to Sex

- What helps her relax?
- Does she like to talk for a while before making love to get her mind off her daily routine? Does she need your encouragement and support in nonsexual matters before she is in tune emotionally for sex?
- Does she enjoy a good massage? Do you know how to give one?
- What type of music does she consider romantic? What kind of music helps make her feel sexy?
- What is the atmosphere that makes her most responsive to or excited for sex? What circumstances in the past have helped made sex special?
- What sort of lighting does she prefer: firelight, candlelight, sunlight, low light, darkness? Has she ever tried to change the lighting in order to make the atmosphere more conducive to sex?
- Does she enjoy scented candles? What scents?
- What times of day is she most responsive to intimacy and pleasure? What is it about that time of day that makes it easiest for her? How can you affect other times of day to help her be more responsive?
- In what places is she most receptive: in bed, in front of the fireplace, in a tent, on a boat? What is it about that situation

that makes her most receptive? How can you affect other situations so that she will be responsive there, as well?

- What style of clothes does she find sexy on you? What clothes does she not like on you? What colors does she like you to wear?
- Does she enjoy creams, lotions, or perfumes rubbed on her skin?
- Does she enjoy having food and drink before, during, and/or after sex?
- Would special sheets (satin, cotton, flannel) make sex more exciting for her?
- Does she enjoy bathing with you?
- Does she like you to watch her undress?
- Where did you meet? Can you re-create that time? Where did you first make love? Can you re-create that situation?
- Recall other satisfying sexual experiences you have had with your partner. Where were they? What made them so good? Can you bring back some aspects of those situations today?
- Recall some of the best sexual experiences with your partner. Are there any similarities in place, time, or other circumstances? Can you re-create those or similar circumstances for the future?
- Does she feel that you want her? How can you let her know that you want her?
- Has she ever asked you to do anything special or different to sexually arouse or excite her?
- Has your partner ever complained about your sex life together? What specifically bothers her? Are her requests reasonable? Are you willing to change your behavior in order to meet her sexual needs?
- Would she be comfortable sharing sexual fantasies with you?
- Do you have a variety of lovemaking styles that excite her (e.g., a quickie style, a slow style, an experimental style)? What are her favorite styles?
- Do you know specifically what gives her sexual pleasure?

- Does she respond to playfulness?
- Does she like you to whisper beautiful things to her when you make love?
- Does she like "rough" sex?
- Does she enjoy "talking dirty?"
- Would she enjoy sharing erotic films or literature when making love?
- Have you told her your sexual desires? Does she want to know your sexual desires?
- Is she uncomfortable with the way she looks or with any part of her body? What can you do to help her feel more comfortable with herself?
- Does she like to initiate sex? What are the circumstances that lead to this?
- After sex, does she enjoy eating, talking, reading, or falling asleep while you hold her?

If She's a Mom

- Does your partner feel exhausted because of work with the children? Does she need time off? Can you help? What is it that she would like you to do?
- Would your partner like some time alone when you arrive home each evening or on weekends so that she can work, read, take a bath, take a walk, or go shopping while you watch the children?
- Does your partner think that you need to spend more time alone with the children so that she has time to herself?
- What activities or hobbies do the children enjoy? What activities or hobbies do you enjoy in which you could include the children? What activities or hobbies of yours could you teach the children to enjoy?
- What camps, cruises, clubs, or other activities can you share as a family, which also allow time away alone with your partner?

- Does your partner feel that you spend enough time together away from the children? Are there particular places she would like to go or things she would like to do with you, away from the children?
- Which baby-sitters does your partner trust? What are their phone numbers?
- Do you know how to find a sitter? Do you know what to know about a sitter before hiring one? Does your partner have a list of important questions to ask to qualify a new sitter? Do you know what responsibilities your partner would like the sitter to take on?
- Do you know neighbors well enough to share "baby-sitting" afternoons, evenings, nights, or weekends?
- What camps or other child-related services can you send the children to for a day, a weekend, or a week away?

Putting It All Together

Now that you know what your partner desires, start making plans to fulfill her desires. Put reminders into your calendar. Go back to earlier chapters and review some of the exercises, and then try them again in light of this new information. And watch her respond.

Grow your romantic spirit. And soon your relationship will glow with romance.

Happily ever after!

Appendix
ROMANCE SURVEY HIGHLIGHTS

Surveys and interviews for this book took place between the fall of 1992 and the summer of 1994, with results compiled continually over that period.

Initially, the authors interviewed dozens of women, and these interviews helped formulate an extensive written survey of over 100 questions. The written survey was followed by posting a shorter electronic version on America Online, Women's Wire, and the Internet. The authors received hundreds of responses from women in their twenties through their seventies living in forty states and Canada.

Responses were highly consistent: after initially analyzing data from about 100 responses, the authors found very little change from data that came from additional responses.

Our Respondents

The survey brought a broad representation in ages of respondents: thirty-five percent were under thirty, thirty-five percent were from ages thirty to thirty-nine, twenty-five percent were from ages forty to sixty, and another five percent were over sixty. Over one-half of the respondents were married, approximately one-third were single, and the remainder were divorced or widowed. Forty-three percent of the responses were from women with children currently living with them. While this was not a scientific survey, the consistency of responses demonstrates that results are representative of heterosexual women across the United States.

Interpretations and synthesis of survey results form the basis of the book. This appendix provides a sampling of the most significant results.

What Is Romance?

The survey listed a number of actions men could take and asked respondents to rate actions from 1 to 5 according to their romantic value, with 5 being the most important to romance. Here are those that received the highest rating.

- He touches me with tenderness (4.7*)
- He snuggles after making love (4.6)
- He treats me as the most special person in his life (4.6)
- He is available when I need help (4.6)
- He gives emotionally (4.5)
- He shares his thoughts and dreams with me (4.5)
- He arranges for us to have time alone (4.4, higher for women with children)
- He knows what makes me happy (4.4)
- He keeps in touch when we are apart (4.4)
- He is gentle in his lovemaking. (4.4)
- He listens to me intently (4.4, higher for married women)
- He treats me special when I am sick or down (4.4)
- He gives me love notes, cards, poems for no special reason (4.3)
- He is playful when we are alone (4.3)
- He undresses me with loving care (4.3)

*The numbers after each item are the averages of responses. Some items had a variation in responses of as much as plus or minus 1.

- He remembers our anniversary or special day (4.2)
- He tells me he loves me (4.2)
- He surprises me with small tokens of love (4.2, higher for women with children)
- He compliments me (4.2, higher for married women)
- He includes me in his plans (4.2)
- He arranges a romantic dinner in or out (4.1)
- He gives me flowers for no special occasion (4.1)
- He initiates spontaneous sex (4.0)

Gifts

In answer to the question "What gifts would you most like to receive?" our respondents provided these suggestions.

- Love, attention, affection, respect, understanding
- Small tokens of affection that demonstrate he is thinking of me
- Jewelry
- Flowers
- Love notes, love letters, his own poetry
- Spontaneous evening or trip just for the two of us that he arranges
- Taking care of things so that I have free time (including certificates for chores he will take care of)
- Books
- Clothes
- Lingerie (primarily mentioned by young, single women)
- Fidelity and honesty forever (single women)
- Tickets to a show or event
- Children (single women)
- Perfume
- Music
- Gift certificate for a massage, facial, or other pampering
- Art
- Pets

What Gets in the Way?

The survey asked, "What gets in the way of romance?" Here are the most common responses:

- Time pressures
- Fatigue
- Work
- Children
- Taking the relationship for granted; falling into a rut
- Problems in the relationship, including lack of communication, emotional commitment
- Stress
- Day-to-day problems and worries (including money)
- Discomfort with being romantic
- Unawareness of the importance of romance to the relationship
- Outside commitments
- Wanting quickie sex
- Geographic distance
- Illness
- TV

What Are Those Little Things That Count?

The survey asked women to list small things that they find romantic. The items they preferred fall into the following categories (in order of preference):

Surprising Her

- Romantic notes, cards, poems, love letters
- Flowers, picked or purchased, a bouquet or a single rose
- Hugging, cuddling, kissing
- Compliments, when we're alone or in front of others
- Candlelight dinner in or out
- Gesture of support and caring

Treating Her Special

- Planning a romantic evening (day, weekend) for just the two of us
- Cooking for me
- Unrequested favors around the house; housecleaning
- Making a bubble bath
- Remembering things I like to do, or eat
- Making morning tea/coffee
- Letting me sleep in
- Flirting/teasing
- Looking into my eyes
- Calling me his pet name for me
- Making me feel sexy even if he's not in the mood for sex
- Helping me accomplish a task he has no interest in
- Photo of me/us in his office
- Delivering lunch to my office and sharing it with me
- Being dropped off and picked up from work
- Dressing up for our dates

Spending Time Together

- Laughter
- Any time alone together
- Walking alone, hand-in-hand
- Dancing
- Being shown something special and private
- Staying in bed together
- Being read to
- Being sung to
- Decorating the Christmas tree
- Sharing chocolate
- Driving in the mountains
- Celebrating our first date

Communicating with Her

- Tells me he loves me
- Tells me I'm beautiful/pretty

- Tells me I drive him crazy
- Calls me to say he's thinking about me
- Asks me about my day
- Conversations about personal things, our future, or anything but work
- Tells me I'm his best friend
- Whispers sweet nothings
- Shares intellectual or philosophical ideas
- Thanks me for doing something for him

Taking Notice

- When I've had a stressful day
- Compliments on how I look
- Telling me I smell good

The Setting

- Watching a sunset
- Walking on the beach or in the woods
- Candlelight
- Firelight
- Music
- Water: shore, lakes
- Soft lighting
- Returning to the place we first met
- Four-poster beds
- Being carried to bed
- Wine

Making Public Private

- Holding my hand when we are out together
- Kissing
- Conspiratorial looks/intimate gazes
- Glances across a crowded room

- Winking at me
- Secret signals
- Being attentive at a gathering
- Whispering something to me that makes me blush in front of others

Touching Her

- Back rubbed, scratched, washed
- Feet rubbed
- Touch of greeting and closeness, such as hug, hand on shoulder, shoulder rub
- Bubble baths or showers together
- Touching my hair: brushing my hair, brushing a strand from my face, or running his hands through
- Kisses on the neck, palm, wrist
- Snuggling/cuddling
- Hand on knee in the car, at a restaurant
- Falling asleep in each other's arms

If He Were More Romantic

The survey asked women "If he were more romantic, I would be more inclined to . . . ? The majority of women responded positively to the following (in order of likelihood):

- Be excited to be with him
- Keep myself looking attractive
- Find out what he wants, try to help him fulfill his needs
- Stay with him rather than find a new partner
- Be in a good mood around him
- Attend to his sexual needs
- Treat him to the sort of outing he likes
- Support his life goals

References

Betcher, William. *Intimate Play* (New York, NY: Penguin Books, 1988).

Campbell, Joseph, with Bill Moyers. *The Power of Myth* (New York, NY: Doubleday, 1988).

Chaucer, Geoffrey. "The Wife of Bath's Tale" from *The Canterbury Tales,* ed., John Halverson (Indianapolis and New York: The Bobbs-Merrill Company, Inc., 1971).

Goldberg, Herb. *The New Male-Female Relationship* (New York, NY: William Morrow and Company, Inc., 1983).

Gray, John. *Men Are from Mars, Women Are from Venus* (New York, NY: HarperCollins, 1992).

Heyn, Dalma. *The Erotic Silence of the American Wife* (New York, NY: Turtle Bay Books, A Division of Random House, Inc., 1992).

Mornell, Pierre. *Passive Men, Wild Women* (New York, NY: Ballantine Books, A Division of Random House, Inc., 1979).

Peck, M. Scott. *The Road Less Traveled* (New York, NY: Simon & Schuster, 1978).

"People Are Hugging a Lot More Now and Seem to Like It," *The Wall Street Journal,* March 15, 1993.

Post, Emily. *Etiquette* (New York, NY: Funk & Wagnalls Company, 1945).

Stoppard, Miriam. *The Magic of Sex* (New York, NY: Dorling Kindersley, Inc. 1992).

Tannen, Deborah. *You Just Don't Understand* (New York, NY: William Morrow and Company, 1990).

Index